DORSET
WITHIN LIVING MEMORY

WITHIN LIVING MEMORY SERIES

Other Counties in the series include:

Bedfordshire	Middlesex
Berkshire	Norfolk
Buckinghamshire	Northamptonshire
Cheshire	Nottinghamshire
Cumbria	Oxfordshire
Derbyshire	Shropshire
Essex	Staffordshire
Gloucestershire	Suffolk
Hampshire	Surrey
Herefordshire	East Sussex
Hertfordshire	Warwickshire
Isle of Wight	West Midlands
East Kent	Wiltshire
West Kent	Worcestershire
Leicestershire & Rutland	North Yorkshire
Lincolnshire	West Yorkshire

DORSET

WITHIN LIVING MEMORY

Compiled by the Dorset Federation
of Women's Institutes from contributions sent by
Institutes in the County

Published jointly by
Countryside Books, Newbury
and the DFWI, Dorchester

First published 1996
© Dorset Federation of Women's Institutes 1996

All rights reserved. No reproduction
permitted without the prior permission
of the publisher:

COUNTRYSIDE BOOKS
3 Catherine Road
Newbury, Berkshire

ISBN 1 85306 404 1

Front cover photograph supplied by Mrs S. Clarke, Stours WI.
Back cover photograph supplied by Mrs J. Horton, Crossways WI.

Produced through MRM Associates Ltd., Reading
Printed by J. W. Arrowsmith Ltd., Bristol

CONTENTS

Sherborne

Beaminster

Maiden Newton

Bridport

Lyme Regis

Abbotsbury

Dorchester

Weymouth

Portland

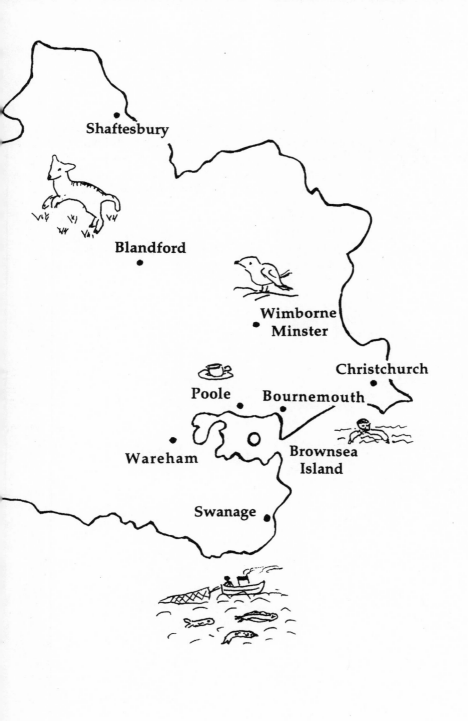

ACKNOWLEDGEMENTS

A sincere thank you to members of the Federation who loaned their treasured photographs and who took time to record traditions, customs and memories of the past. It gave me so much pleasure to read the material submitted and it was all tremendous value to 'Within Living Memory'. Unfortunately not all photographs and articles could be included.

Particular thanks are extended to Sally Roper for her beautiful silhouette drawings, to Philip Roper for permission to use material from *Boyhood Memories of Bridport Harbour 1920–1939*, and to members of the County House staff, Carol, Lisa, Rosanne and Valerie.

Jean Horton
Co-ordinator

FOREWORD

Dorset, the setting for the stories and anecdotes in this book, is geographically divided into three parts – the heathlands of the east, the rolling chalk downs of the centre, and the hills and secret valleys of the west. It is bordered in the north by the A303, and in the south by rugged cliffs, tiny coves, and the great sweep of the Chesil Beach.

It has been remarkably untouched by the 20th century, there being only one conurbation, and that on its south-eastern fringe.

Although Dorset has always been a farming county, in more recent times, men, usurped by machinery, have left the land to look for new work in the towns. But the land itself, the network of lanes, the villages and market towns, have remained much as they were in earlier days.

Next to farming, tourism is now probably the most important industry in a county that offers beauty, peace and tranquillity to the tens of thousands of holidaymakers who visit the area from spring to autumn every year.

We thank all the members of the Dorset Federation of Women's Institutes who have painstakingly recorded the stories and pictures of everyday life, of occasions great and small, happy and sad. We also thank Jean Horton who has patiently gathered the material to make an important chronicle of the social history of the county during this century.

Judy Livingstone
County Chairman

TOWN&COUNTRY LIFE

Some Towns and Villages Remembered

Country lanes along which passed only the occasional farm cart; lamplighters and street traders; working harbours and peaceful beaches – just some of the memories we share of Dorset within living memory.

▣ Bournemouth in the 1920s ▣

'Life started for me on the 21st day of December 1916 – what a Christmas present for my parents as they had been blessed with three girls before my arrival and now a son and heir. There is quite a story about this date as my father was due to attend at Winchester Military Barracks for his medical examination for war service that morning. He failed, possibly due to the rushed anxious moments. It seems there was a mad rush around to get the midwife (usually a near neighbour in those days) before running to catch the train at the West Station – yes, he ran because transport direct to certain areas was not conveniently available as now but trams were running on some major routes. His dash was from the Winton area of Bournemouth where my parents lived with my maternal grandfather.

My childhood years were very happy ones, five girls and four boys and we were a very close family, but as our house had only three bedrooms the elder girls on leaving school went into domestic service living in. In those days there were many more of the larger houses, wealthier folks who employed permanent live-in servants – cooks, chambermaids, housekeepers, parlourmaids etc – and generally with a chauffeur and gardeners. Typical of these were on both sides of Wimborne Road from Richmond Hill to Cemetery Junction and beyond.

I can remember starting school when I was three at St Luke's infants' school which was only a short distance from our house, situated on the corner of Latimer Road and Wimborne Road (now the main shopping area of Winton) and the site where the original St Luke's church stood. Opposite the school was the Co-Operative Wholesale Society stores and on the other side of Wimborne Road we watched the blacksmith at work, principally shoeing horses as these were still being used in considerable numbers. My father had a pony stabled with one other larger horse in stable buildings opposite our house. You can still see many of these old stable buildings in some areas of Bournemouth with current day uses. The blacksmith – how can I forget that distinctive smell of smoke as the smith held, with large tongs, the red-hot iron shoe (plate), fitted it to the horse's hoof and finally nailed it, twisting off the protruding end of the nail. In cold frosty weather he did not object to us warming ourselves by the

Selling fish from a cart on the streets of Bournemouth in the 1920s.

forge, brought to life by the large bellows. My father's cart was pulled by the pony for his fish round, but it was with a donkey when he started.

Local shops included grocers Williamson & Treadgold and Hudsons Brudenells for fruit. The Cadena Cafe was always good for cakes (this was where my grandfather had his weekly supply of coffee and chicory) and at Robsons at the Triangle there was always that wonderful aroma of the coffee being ground and prepared. I almost forgot, probably the oldest store in town, Beale's, now a very large department store, was good on occasion for "broken" toys.

The Bournemouth Labour Exchange was adjacent to the school and we looked down from the boys' playground to the long lines of unemployed men queuing for jobs or the dole. My sister recalls the queue extending out of the building and along Yelverton Road, passing Granville Chambers and right back to Richmond Hill – a sad sight in the times of recession in the early to mid 1920s.

The two entrances to the school were opposite to the rear of the Theatre Royal and a favourite pastime for we small boys (little horrors!) was to retrieve the many rejected electric light bulbs, from the footlights presumably, and smash them against the wall with a satisfying loud bang. Electricity was modern then as many public buildings and homes still had gas lighting. Street lighting was also gas and the lamplighter would come round in the evening and either climb the lamp-post or ascend on a short ladder he carried hung over his shoulder (even though he rode a cycle on his round) to turn on the gas to the mantle from the pilot lights. I suppose he turned it off again in the morning, one of the actions carried out by men early, "before the streets were aired" as my mother used to say.

My grandfather and father rented a large allotment in Talbot Woods where the West Hants Tennis Club courts are situated today and it was our treat at weekends and bank holidays to go there and play in the woods and long grass whilst vegetable gardening proceeded. It was always a serious discussion round the kitchen table, annually, with my grandad and dad deciding what seeds, seed potatoes etc were needed for full production in the large rear garden at home and in the allotment, as growing our own was essential to help with the family budget. At the bottom of our garden my mother kept chickens, hatching her own chicks from eggs obtained from neighbours. When eggs were plentiful she preserved some in waterglass in a large earthenware container.

I mentioned earlier the extensive use of horses. Close to home was the corporation yard with stables for the many large carthorses (beautiful creatures – my favourite). They were used to pull all vehicles, including dust carts and water carts for spraying roads, as many roads were still rolled gravel surfaces. Of course, horses were used by undertakers to pull the hearse and carriages for the mourners, in fact my grandfather's funeral in 1932 was arranged as such by the Pike Family Funeral Services, Winton who continued for many years after.

The existence of horses was a boon for small boys (and not so small boys) collecting the manure from the roads for the garden, with bucket and shovel or a small home-made cart made up on old pram wheels. There was always a small gathering outside the corporation yard when the many horses came out very early in the morning to start work for the day. My two brothers after me had a little pocket money "business" running. It's related that they sold a bucket of manure for sixpence and the older one sent his younger brother into the house asking the lady the required purchase price, sixpence. He came out with only twopence, "All she would pay," he said, whereupon he was immediately despatched back to return the twopence and to re-bucket the product. As is to be expected, the older one

proved to be a real businessman with two of his own retail fruit and vegetable shops locally in later years.

Lastly on horses, the shout "Whip behind, mister" was often used to warn the driver a youngster was stealing a ride on the back. There were many street traders shouting their wares and services, for instance fish rounds (as my father), bakers, hardware goods, paraffin etc, "scissors to grind", "knives to grind", "rag-&-bone", barrel organs with monkeys on top and, particularly on Sunday afternoons, water-cress in season, mackerel, herring and sprats, generally from Poole. There were also annual visits by Frenchmen in summer with strings of onions.

Light evenings were spent in the street outside our homes with boys in the immediate vicinity: football perhaps, with a small ball (named a "pill"), with a look-out for the local bobby coming through every evening. We had great respect for him or a clip round the ear would be forthcoming. Hide and seek was played in the gardens of the whole block of houses, not forgetting pranks such as "pin tick", with a length of cotton and a button tapping the windows whilst we hid behind the front wall, or the purse on the pavement attached to string which we pulled around the corner at the moment the poor lady stooped to pick it up.

On Sundays, with the family all together, there was always a good roast dinner with perhaps a large joint of beef costing about two shillings and sixpence (a half a crown). All the children had their tasks, mine normally to peel lots of potatoes, but one of my brothers shared in making the cake and pastries with my older sisters. Another task for me was an errand to the nearby off-licence for a quart flagon of "Old" beer for Dad and Grandad and I recall seeing flakes of hops floating on top. Of course, the law required the bottle to have a strip paper label over the stopper to ensure the child collecting could not drink some on the way home.

In those days there was only one cinema in Winton, later called the Plaza and finally the Continental for many years but recently demolished. It was silent films in those early days and a pianist played music which was appropriate to the action showing on screen.'

'At the beginning of the 20th century Sutton Poyntz was a small hamlet, consisting of three farms, farm cottages and a sprinkling of cottages round the pond and along the banks of the river Jordan which wound through the valley to Preston and Bowleaze Cove. Most cottages were thatched, with thick stone walls. To the north rose the smooth outline of the Ridgeway but the valleys were dense with elm trees.

Both Sutton Poyntz and Preston were part of the Weld estate. The inhabitants paid their ground rent annually at the court house with a constable in charge of the proceedings and a jury. Each juryman was paid eightpence so the job was quite popular. The court was advertised by a man going round at midnight, a few days before it sat, ringing a bell.

Sutton was a peaceful place with the country lanes bordered by little streams and only an occasional farm cart passing along them. Children played hopscotch, marbles and hoops in the road with no disturbance. Primroses and bluebells abounded in the copses and cowslips in many of the fields. No tractors, just carthorses winding slowly up and down the fields. Sheep grazed on the hillsides making little paths for children to run along. The hills were covered with wild flowers.

Preston, the adjoining village, contained the church, appropriately dedicated to St Andrew, the fisherman. In the times that I am writing about, it was in a very picturesque setting between two farms overlooking the sea at beautiful Bowleaze with the Isle of Portland and Weymouth Bay in view. Near the church stood the school which in those days was an attractive building consisting of three classrooms heated by open fires and the infants' room which had a tortoise stove. About a hundred children attended from the ages of five to 14. The children learnt the three Rs, also needlework, knitting and woodwork. Scripture was taught each morning by the vicar. The original building still exists but it has been enlarged beyond recognition.

The fields to the south of Preston were water meadows and in bygone days they had been criss-crossed with ditches with hatches at various points to control the water. Bowleaze Cove was a very quiet and lovely bay visited only by the village people for picnics. They lit fires on the beach and obtained fresh water from the cliffs. There was no approach road, one wandered through fields of waving corn to get there. It is very different now. Gone are the cornfields and the sheep and most of the cows, now the quiet fields of Preston are covered with caravans and estates of new houses.

Life in those days was in some ways much easier than now. Sutton Poyntz had a blacksmith, a wheelwright and a carpenter. In Preston there was a stonemason and a cobbler. Shops were a grocer's, butcher's and baker's, and there was also a sweetshop. Bread was delivered every day except Sunday and meat was delivered three times a week. Most of the villagers fetched their milk from the farms, children going to the cowshed and waiting until the dairyman had finished milking a cow and could serve them. Fresh milk, then, warm from the cow.

Lime was quarried from Chalbury Hill and until quite recently the ruins of the lime kiln could be seen on the side of the hill. It was a favourite walk from Sutton; the villagers would say, "We've been up round lime kiln." From the hills to the north of Plaisters Lane chalk was quarried. We always called that part of the hill Chalk Pit. Nowadays it is full of garages, then it was full of jackdaws' nests.

There were three mills on the river Jordan, one at Sutton Poyntz (which is still there, but no longer in use) and two in Preston, which have now been replaced by houses.

In the days of which I am writing families looked after their own graves so there was no need for volunteers to do this task. Every Saturday and Sunday afternoon there would be a crowd of relatives in the churchyard tending the graves and exchanging gossip, it was quite a social occasion.

Before the Weld estate was broken up there was a huge rookery in Plaisters Lane and a rook shoot was held each May. After the sale of the estate the elm trees were cut down and all the rooks left.'

✦ MELBURY ABBAS IN THE 1900S ✦

'I was born in Melbury Abbas in 1899 during a blizzard. My father had to walk three miles to Shaftesbury to get the doctor, who came out on horseback. I have lived in that cottage, or this one in the same row all my life, the accommodation being "two up and two down".

Times were hard. My mother used to make trousers for my brother and I, from the backs of my father's old ones. Pay day was Saturday, every 14 days and sometimes as late as 8 pm, so the shopping was done on Saturday nights, with a three mile walk to Shaftesbury. The shops stayed open until 11 pm. I can't remember what the local weekly paper (1d a week), was called. We called it the Penny Liar. We couldn't afford a national paper at 1d a day. My mother made all our own bread. We kept two pigs, one to eat and one to sell. We cured our own bacon and grew all our own vegetables and some fruit in our large garden and also my father had an allotment.

I remember the "young" Sir Richard Glyn starting up a village Rifle Club in 1911. My brother, three years older than me, joined, but I couldn't until I was 14. I don't know if Sir Richard was thinking of the First World War then and wanted the men to be good shots. But we always thought that it was so afterwards, because a good many of those men went to the war.

I don't remember ever going to the doctor and I don't go now. Of course, you had to pay. It was hard do's they sometimes didn't have the doctor when they needed to. I never bothered about teeth and never went to the dentist. There were no school dentists.

When people died there was no cremation then and it didn't cost very much for a funeral. The dead stayed in the house. The coffin was carried on the shoulders to the church. I used to act as bearer and I've carried a fair few on my shoulder for a good many miles.

People in those days were good neighbours. I remember in the summer time when the men came home from work they used to go and work in the garden and when they had finished they would all sit down together. Then one of them would bring out a jug of ale. In those days you could get an 18 gallon barrel of ale at 10d a gallon. The best ale was 1s a gallon. If a woman was ill, one of the next door neighbours would cook a meal for the children and the husband. They did it for each other.

When the 1914 war came, I was 15. A lot of men including my brother volunteered to join up straight away. This was in August and they thought it would be over by Christmas. I don't think they thought about being wounded or killed. I volunteered in 1917. They sent me for a medical to Dorchester and chucked me out, just like that ... irregular heart they said. I'm doing alright now with an irregular heart! The doctor called in the colonel who said, "You're no good to us, you can do more good there on the farm than you can for us." I was lucky. The day I was having my medical, was the same day as my brother was killed, 2nd April 1917. We didn't hear it until about a week afterwards when we had a telegram. In 1915 he had pneumonia and Father and Mother went out to France to see him because he wasn't expected to live. He got over that and came home and they said that he would never have to go out to France again. He was only back in the depot in Dorchester a week when he was sent back out there again and then he was killed. Quite a lot of the men were killed, it caused great shock in the village. Otherwise we didn't really know that the war was on. There were no bomb scares or anything and there was no "Dad's Army", as in the second war. Life went on as normal; the farmers were more prosperous and wages went up to 36s a week for labourers and cowmen, stockmen and carters had 52s.

There was a time when we made cider, which was then drunk more than ale. At Cann Mill we made thousands of gallons of cider which went to all the farmers round. At one time, this row of cottages was a brewery. They made beer for the district. When these buildings were turned into cottages the man who bought them paid £50 each for them, £250 for the five.

I can't remember when we first had a wireless. I know it was before the Second World War. The wireless didn't make much difference to us. When we got home from work we always had to do the garden or something. By the time we had done that and had a bit of supper, we went to bed. You see that television there, I don't watch it. I get books from the library and I read them.

When the war came, I joined the Home Guard, but I might as well have not, because we didn't have any weapons. After a time we had six rifles and a gun that fired bombs. We were trained to use that and I was a lance corporal in charge of it. I remember we went to Bovington and had to fire it at tanks coming up over the hill. I gave the order to fire and the first three shots hit the track in front of the tanks. The officer told me to raise the sight and the next shot went over the top of the tank. I told the officer that hitting the track was more likely to stop them. He said I was right and that he wouldn't interfere with me again.

The real changes in the village happened just after the war. Different people came to live in the village and some moved out. The fresh people who came in, didn't know you and you didn't know them. As people died, their children didn't take over from them as they used to. They went away. People were having smaller families too. There was no work here, or in Shaftesbury except farming and building. They moved away to where there was work. Television has killed the village a lot. We used to have socials and dances and so on. The three pubs closed, I don't think they had the trade. There wasn't the traffic that there is now.'

▨ STUDLAND BEACH ▨

'No cars or vehicles of any description were allowed on Studland Beach till the late 1940s. There were large ponds on either side of the road leading to the beach, now covered in and used as car parks. There was a beach inspector on Studland Beach up to the closing of the beach in late summer 1940, after Dunkirk. Up until then no undressing was allowed on the beach, beach huts being provided for that purpose. In the 1920s, no man was allowed on the beach in bathing trunks; if a costume was rolled down the inspector pointed with his sergeant major's pacing stick: "Pull that costume up young man, at once!" Many times the inspector could be seen with clothes tucked under his arm, conveying them to his look-out office, to be claimed by distraught young men or women who would be brusquely but politely directed to the row of beach huts where they could dress.

The sand dunes we loved were much bigger then, and hide and seek a favourite game. Our children played there in the 1950s and 1960s, happily laughing and climbing, and enjoying the Mount Everest, the highest one, lovely carefree hours.'

▨ WEYMOUTH IN THE 1920s ▨

'My father, who was in the Navy, retired from his last appointment at Portland dockyard in 1923. Liking Dorset, he bought a house in Weymouth for his retirement, situated in Mount Pleasant Avenue.

Decorum was maintained on Studland Beach by an inspector up to the 1940s.

It was one of only four houses in the road at that time, a five bed-roomed house for which my father paid £1,000! It had its drawbacks, having no lighting except oil lamps and coal fires with a huge range in the kitchen. Enquiries were made as to whether electricity could be

A wreck off Swanage in 1908, a reminder of the sea's power along our coastline.

installed and we were told that the main only reached as far as the Spa Hotel and it would cost £500 to run it up to Mount Pleasant. Back in those days that was quite a large sum, so as gas was available gas was put in for heating and lighting, and with that we had to be content until electricity came up to Manor Road in the middle 1930s.

Manor Road was at that time the northern boundary of Weymouth, it was not until 1934 that it was extended to the top of Ridgeway Hill. There were no houses beyond Mount Pleasant until reaching Nottingham Corner except for Redlands Farm. All the land was open fields.

After my father retired he wanted something to occupy his time so in due course he became a town councillor. He got interested in the development of Radipole Lake and became chairman of the committee dealing with it.

Originally Radipole Park Drive was a mudbank. A dredger was hired to dig out the bottom of the lake and pile it up to form a solid ridge upon which the road was built. There was water either side of it as the lake originally went right up to the railway line. So between the new road and the railway the space was gradually filled in and the present gardens and tennis courts were laid out.

There was no car park at Westham Bridge, the water came right up to the road. My father objected to town rubbish being put into the lake. However, as soon as he retired from the council those that followed him immediately started town refuse being dumped thus reclaiming what is now the car park.

So many changes since those days. The esplanade was half its present width. There were no ornamental gardens in front of the statue, just open road space with a rather dingy bus shelter in the middle. Open charabancs used to wait there to take visitors for trips. A trip to Abbotsbury was quite an adventure! There was one horse-drawn brake that plied for hire to and fro to Upwey Wishing Well driven by an old character – Sugaram Shorey. This old man lived in a cottage on the Preston Road halfway between Greenhill and Overcombe Corner, the only building along that road. It has been gone many years now. There were no houses from Overcombe Corner until you reached Littlemoor Road, except for one farm, and there were only two houses on the road to Bowleaze Cove.

The Navy *was* a navy in those days. Portland harbour had many great battleships and cruisers anchored there, as well as numbers of smaller craft. Weymouth saw many sailors ashore in the evening, all in uniform.'

▩ PORTLAND LIFE ▩

'Portland, almost an island and joined to the mainland by the famous Chesil Beach, had Portland harbour and dockyard and naval school, HMS *Osprey*, the Verne Citadel, occupied at times by Dorset's Lincoln and Green Howards, the Borstal institution, the lighthouse and Coast-guard stations. But the local industry was stone; we grew up to the clink of metal on stone, the warm steamy smell of traction engines which pulled the famous Portland stone. I remember the great ruts of mud they left on the road. Then came the depression and the mill and the quarries were almost stilled, men were unemployed and on the means test; those with no commitments went to Jersey digging potatoes or picking tomatoes.

My family lived in the Grove. The community always seemed very close. At school we had lady teachers who were extremely strict but very fair. St Peter's church, the Catholic church and Gospel Hall were well used. St Peter's was the garrison church and every fourth Sunday the regiment would march to church, and after the service, march down the Grove up Easton Lane and across New Ground with the band playing, and if you wished you could enter the barracks, where the band would play on the square. The Fleet often assembled in the harbour and we would gather on the incline to watch a searchlight display on a summer evening.

There were two really big highlights for us. One was the Sunday school outing, when we would be taken in a charabanc to Upwey to a field on Mr Comben's farm, or Abbotsbury, and once Springhead! The other was Portland Fair. We used to scrub the front steps and basement stairs for threepence, which we saved for these two occasions.

In the summer our days were spent on Little Beach. We'd take a bottle of water flavoured with lemonade powder, and sandwiches, then spend the whole day swimming and fishing. Girls one side of the beach, boys the other was the rule strictly followed, on whichever beach we visited. We were free to wander through the fields, and a favourite walk was down the East Weares where primroses peeped from under the stones. There was a frog pond to visit or perhaps we'd go to Underhill Common and walk through the Verne Road and look for orchids. We also liked to visit the Naval cemetery and put some wild flowers on the sailors' graves.

In the autumn we'd play on the mound opposite, sliding down the side on a piece of galvanised iron. Dark evenings we played ludo, snakes and ladders or draughts, and of course we had our Brownies and Guides.

Christmas and Easter were festive times when families gathered together; there would always be Christmas pudding or cake and the families' own recipe Portland dough cake and rice cake. As nearly every family had an allotment and kept a few chickens, home-made pickled onions and eggs, beetroot and cabbage would be sampled.

Groceries, milk and bread were brought to the door, the milk in big churns, doled out into your jug; it was lovely and creamy to drink. I remember once the horse that pulled the cart bolted in Grove Road and churns and milk went all over the road. We thought it was quite funny at the time.'

◼ BRIDPORT HARBOUR BETWEEN THE WARS ◼

'My first recollection of Bridport harbour is of living in a wooden bungalow in the north-west corner of the old shipyard which was where the 40 Foot Way joins the West Cliff estate. Although the coming of the railway introduced the name "West Bay" the locals always retained the old name, and the road leading to the harbour was known as Harbour Road for some years.

There was another bungalow next door occupied by one Roy Knight and the land to the south was allotments. Around the edge of the shipyard were a number of bungalows and two large stone houses occupied by a Mr Tresize and a Mr Hare, also among those living in the shipyard was a Mr Ned Forsey one of the last survivors of the old shipbuilding days – a fine figure of a man with a white beard who had lost one of his thumbs in an accident. When the piers were lined with wooden piles it was he who shaped the pointed ends with an adze. Descendants of his still live in Bridport.

There were very few days when there was not at least one ship in the harbour. They were then all sail, consisting of small coasting

West Street, Bridport early in the century and after the Second World War.

schooners and ketches, Thames barges and larger ships from the Baltic countries, mostly Danish, Swedish and German. Very few had auxiliary engines and they had to be manhandled in by a capstan situated outside the black hut on the east pier. They brought in a variety of cargoes such as timbers, cattle cake, cement, coal, and stone from the Channel Islands for roads. Cargoes were discharged by the ships' own derricks powered by donkey engines.

Timber ships invariably carried deck cargo which was unloaded by hand and most of those involved spent the evenings taking out splinters. Ships then would berth alongside the North and South quays of the harbour as well as the Crane House berth where trawlers and visiting yachts now berth, and timber was hauled away by long horse-drawn carts. The various warehouses were in George Street and on the sites where now stand Chesil Court, Harbour House and St John's church, which was built in 1931. Some of the timber was taken away by train. Cement was unloaded in bags, and coal and stone in large baskets, which were discharged into waiting horse-drawn carts and carried away.

Many of the ships having discharged would load with gravel, and their stay in port was much longer than today. When they left harbour, unless they had an auxiliary engine or there was a northerly wind they were towed out by the *Rake*, a fishing boat owned by Mr Albion Whetham and skippered by Frank Butt, who was later to become Trinity House pilot for the harbour. There was another similar boat in the harbour, the *Lucky Dip*, owned by Dr Ryan of Burton Bradstock and skippered by Tom Swaffield. One of the first boats to take passengers for "trips round the bay" was the *Delaware* which was said to have been left behind by an American warship of the same name after the First World War. It was skippered by Bill Hawkins, a naval pensioner, later to be steward at the golf club.

During the summer months, Cozens of Weymouth ran paddle steamer trips from Weymouth to Torquay, calling at Bridport en route. There were two steamers, *Victoria* and *Alexandra*, and weather permitting (which it always seemed to be!) they called on Tuesdays and

Thursdays to pick up for Torquay in the morning and return in the evening.

If there was enough water they would berth between the piers and if not they would run bow on to the East Beach and rig a gangway from ship to shore to enable passengers to board and/or disembark. They would stream a stern anchor to pull the ship off. Despite being very seaworthy, if it blew up during the day, they would return direct to Weymouth.

In those days, a lot of seine fishing was done all along the Chesil Beach with crews of about half a dozen and mostly in lerrets or double ended boats which could more easily be launched from and landed on the beach. One of the crew was usually stationed on the cliff top looking for "Mackel Strayen". When he saw a shoal of mackerel near the beach he would alert the crew who would launch the boat, pay out the net over the stern, row round the shoal and return to the beach. One end of the net would have been left with one of the crew on the beach and then both ends would be hauled in with hopefully a good catch.

There was then a flourishing sailing club; the West Bay Corinthian Sailing Club with its headquarters on the first floor of the pavilion

which stood on the Mound where the harbour master's office and adjacent car park are now situated, which was washed away in 1942.

The swimming club hut then stood on the West pier and the polo ground was nearby, but has now been enclosed by the rebuilding of the pier. Depending on the state of the tide, matches would be played there or in the river and sometimes in the harbour just in front of the sluices. The referee was Mr Louis Trevett, a local hairdresser and tobacconist.

Many dozens of local children were taught to swim by my father and others, suspended on a belt from the jetty which was on the east side of the polo ground.

My father's love of the water and swimming strength reminds me of one of the most notably courageous events at the harbour, which took place in September 1920, although I was too young actually to remember this event. In conditions of near gale force winds and a rough sea, a Weymouth trawler, *The Seagull* – skipper, Jack Northover, a Weymouth fisherman, with, on board one Richard Price of Bath and his twelve year old son – capsized while attempting to enter the harbour. My father witnessed this from the West pier and despite the conditions dived into the sea. He managed to reach the boy, release him from the wreckage and swim with him to the East pier where a large wave lifted him sufficiently high for him to be snatched to safety by onlookers. Unfortunately both Northover and Price were drowned. For this courageous act, my father was awarded the Royal Humane Society's Bronze Medal.

The great event of the year for both sailors and swimmers, was regatta week held during the first week of August. Regatta day was always the Thursday (early closing) with sailing races in the morning, swimming and diving in the afternoon, with a motor boat race in the evening.

The harbour now has no ships coming in. The coastal trade was largely taken over in the 1930s by Dutch and German motor vessels. Planners have decreed that the extraction of gravel from the Chesil Beach should cease and gravel is no longer exported by sea.

A prominent local family was the Goods who were first appointed Lloyd's agents in 1828. The first holder of this office was John Bools Good who was also harbour master, being recommended by his predecessor who described him as "an active and intelligent person well acquainted with ships".

Mr Norman Good was appointed in 1903 and also ran the family business of sand and gravel merchants. In addition, members of the Good family were sub-commissioners for pilotage appointed by Trinity House. Sadly, after several hundred years, coastal pilotage has been removed from Trinity House and transferred to local authorities. Another link with the past has gone with the banning of gravel extraction from the Chesil Beach. Pea gravel, as it is known, was exported all over the world by Norman Good & Sons, mostly by sea.

Apart from the train service there was very little public transport between the harbour and town. Mr Kitcher ran a grey bus and there were a few taxis known as the "threepennies", which was the cost of the journey between the town and the harbour.

Later the National buses started a service which included a "toast rack", a slow-moving small-wheeled vehicle with transverse seats. Traffic was so scarce that when the road was first asphalted it was perfectly safe to roller skate up and down. The West cliff extended very much further to seaward and another favourite pastime was to take a bicycle to the stile at the top and race down over two "jumps" about halfway down, turning right at the bottom where the slope was sufficient to bring you to a stop without using brakes.

During the summer we used to get visits from Alan Cobham's Flying Circus, usually a couple of open cockpit two-seater biplanes which took off from what is now the Melplash Show field; once round the harbour 5s, a longer circuit for 10s and for £1 loop the loop!'

▩ CHILD OKEFORD IN THE 1940s ▩

'There were two public houses and a stream ran along the street. I am told quite a few came out of the Royal Oak in the blackout during the war and ended up in the stream.

There was a post office cum general store which even had a library. There was a village hall and a temperance hall; there was quite an active temperance society at one time. The church had a good congregation on Sundays and the rectory was quite a big house which was very cold in the winter, just a fire going in a big room, no central heating. The Rev Mortimer died tragically in 1956 when he was showing some children the bells in the belfry one Sunday after the service. It appears the bell had been left in an up position and it swung down and killed him instantly; he left a wife and grown up daughter and son. I remember lovely Nativity plays in the church, my son wearing a striped towel. Every year a group of us would go carol singing and the money would be used for coal for the pensioners. We used to borrow a low trolley from the factory and a Miss Wallace would play a harmonium which was perched on it; we used to get a few strong boys to pull her around. We used to creep up to the big houses and burst into song. Some of the old boys would whip out their hip flasks and have a quick nip to keep out the cold.

One other thing I remember, wellington boots were scarce just after the war and the milk factory workers were all supplied with clogs.'

▨ HALSTOCK IN THE 1920s ▨

'In the 1920s the life of the village centred around the church, the school and the farms. Families were generally much larger and when the school bell rang at 8.50 am, from all over the village children hurried to school, on foot in all weather conditions, from Halstock Leigh and the Closworth and Corscombe roads. The writers remember 21 children from two homes, running down the road together from Halstock Leigh and playing on the way "till they were late"! School was popular, especially the craft lessons and the daily visit of the rector, the Rev Plater who took the Scripture lesson.

On special saints days, the children went along to the church. They were taught to go to church three times each Sunday – to the morning service, to Sunday school in the afternoon and to evensong.

Each Saturday Mr Crabb lit the coke stove to heat the church for Sunday and stoked it several times before the services began on Sunday. His wife each week cleaned and fitted the brass oil lamps which lit the church. During services the lamps sometimes smoked and anyone nearby would promptly get up and turn down the wick.

The children liked singing in the choir and pumping the organ which was then at the east end of the north aisle. Each year there was a Sunday school outing in which the children who attended the little chapel – or Gospel Hall – joined, and this was a day trip by coach to the sea at Weymouth, a great treat for them all.

Many of the houses in the village at that time were thatched and there was plenty of work for two thatchers on roofs and ricks. The village was almost self contained, having at its centre two shops, a post office, bakery, cobbler, carpenter and undertaker, blacksmith and two public houses and a travelling threshing machine.

There was then no electricity or piped water. One of our writers remembers drinking water being carried home each evening by her uncle from his work at Harvard Farm, in two buckets slung from a wooden yoke across his shoulders; his home was near St Mary's church. The water for cleaning purposes came from pumps often shared among several cottages in the village.

There were many farm workers in those days and of course horses, but few cars. Shopping trips to Yeovil were made in pony carts or on foot, sometimes pushing the children in a pram, or the elderly and infirm in a wheelchair. For funerals the village bier was used and a gravedigger hired in the village.

The reservoir had not then been constructed at Sutton Bingham and the approach to the village was narrow and more twisting than it is today.

Beginning at the top of Adams Green Hill, there was a cottage which no longer exists, but then was the home of Emanuel Edis, and below this a new building replaced the wooden bungalow that was the home of the village cobbler, Joshua Loveless. The only water supply to those two cottages was from a spring in the field opposite where a pipe ran from the spring to the tank in the hedge.

Below this were two cottages with thatched roofs. Elisa and William Abbott lived next door to each other and they were both thatchers. Below these cottages lived an elderly man by the name of Charlie Rossiter and at one time he carried on the bakery in the village. In the 1920s the area around The Quiet Woman was owned by Lord Ilchester.

Beside the New Inn is Common Lane, which leads to Corscombe. There used to be an old cottage built of mud and stone some distance from the village, which was unusual in having a staircase on the outside. Pat and Martha Bartlett lived there and they used to travel about the village in a donkey cart.

The post office in those days was in "The Little House", and the village stores opened at 8 am and closed again at 9 pm, six days a week. Mrs Manual owned the stores and her daughter was one of the teachers at the village school.

The house later known as The Old House was another shop and belonged to Mr and Mrs Lane, who owned a threshing machine which travelled to the many neighbouring farms and was worked by Mr Barnet Dodge who was the father of Mrs Riggs.

The village carpenter and undertaker was Mr William Clarke, who lived in the cottage adjoining the little chapel. When he died his son, Mr Frank Clarke, continued the family business. The village blacksmith was a Mr Hallett who lived and worked at Forge Cross.

On the outskirts of the village lay the mill and corn was brought there to be ground from the villages around. The narrow lane which was the approach to the mill from Pendomer no longer exists as such.'

❖ West Lulworth Changes ❖

'I came to West Lulworth in 1943, and at first it would appear that nothing much has changed.

Even the war years were quiet, though we had a military training camp just up the hill, and not many local men were called up as many jobs were reserved occupations.

Doctors from Wool and Wareham would come out when called, and there was a surgery held occasionally in the little thatched cottage next to the Central garage.

Milk deliveries were made by a farmer who brought it in a churn and ladled it out into our containers. Not so hygienic as the present method! Mr Dorey had the grocer's shop next to the village hall, and prior to this his mother ran a shop further up the village. Mr William Chaffey was our coalman.

Most of our children started their education at the village school – then with two female teachers. Things changed considerably when Mr Hollowood took over and children were coached to go on to Swanage grammar school (if they were brainy enough!). Eventually Bovington school was built and children went on there until they were 16 years old, until the new school at Wareham was built.

Visitors and cars started to come in greater numbers about 1956. Providing facilities for them created many more jobs for local people, as did Lulworth and Bovington military camps, which became permanent military training establishments and created many types of civilian jobs for the area.'

❖ Dorset Characters ❖

'My grandfather, six feet tall and 18 stone in weight, was a colourful character. Born at Cann Common, Shaftesbury in 1863, he experienced the hardships of rural life during his childhood, and the Victorian years thereafter. He became a dealer, and in 1913 a farmer. His first wife died in childbed, leaving four small children. Some ten years later, his second marriage ended when he found his wife dead of a heart attack.

At the age of 62 he married a third time, to a 36 year old bride, a young lady who had spent her life as a lady's maid to a local aristocratic family.

During the early 1920s Grandfather was in the village of Kington Magna on business, and enjoying a pint at mid-day in the village inn.

Kington Magna was the village home of his new wife, and he was soon in conversation with the locals. Asking questions to which he already knew the answers, he asked someone, "Whatever happened to a Miss Coombes who was employed as a lady's maid to Lady Wynford for some years?" "Oh! she's married now" shouted some loud mouth. "Married a bloody great fat farmer up Shaftesbury way, old enough to be her father."

"Shake hands," said Grandad, "I'm the man she married"!'

'In the 1920s, I came to know Mr Walter Brockway quite well. He was retired of course, but kept busy at his hobby of breeding and fattening pigs in his orchard, opposite his tiny thatched cottage, below Zig Zag hill. My father, a dealer, purchased most of his production, and we were often there loading pigs on their way to market.

My father told me the following story. When Walter was a young man and newly married, he and his wife had a domestic upset, which resulted in Walter's wife leaving him, and claiming maintenance through the court.

Walter was damned if he would pay her one penny, and in due course had to appear at Dorchester court, where he was found guilty of non-payment, and was sentenced to 28 days' hard labour. This, he spent in the garden of the prison governor there. He continued to

serve this sentence annually, for several years, and he and the prison governor became friends.

When notified to attend, Walter would visit my grandfather and arrange a lift in his waggon to the Three Choughs Inn at Blandford, used as a staging post for waggons at that time, where arrangements were made to transport Walter on to Dorchester with another carrier.

I never knew Mrs Brockway personally, but recently, when transcribing the burial register of Melbury Abbas church, I came across the burial of Walter G. Brockway, at the ripe old age of 87 and just alongside the burial of Louisa Brockway, from the same address as Walter, at Zig Zag corner, and a year or so younger. So it seems they got back together again after all, and lived happily ever after!'

'My mother told us many stories of the past, but the one that intrigued me the most was of her encounter with T. E. Lawrence, better known as Lawrence of Arabia. She was first introduced to him by her brother-in-law who owned the Garage Red Hill, now known as Garrison Garage in Bovington. My uncle serviced Lawrence's Brough Superior motor cycle and was also his banker.

Eventually, Uncle Roy brought Lawrence home to meet his parents-in-law (my grandparents), who lived at The Farmhouse at Winfrith. He became a frequent visitor for Sunday afternoon tea and this led to a friendship with my mother. She rode pillion on his motorbike many times. My mother drove her father's Ford Model T car and often drove Lawrence up to London to attend various meetings. During one of these trips my mother was introduced to George Bernard Shaw, the author and playwright, but I cannot recall much about this.

Many years later, my brother was working as a taxi driver and was sent to collect an American gentleman from Wool station. He wished to go and visit Lawrence of Arabia's grave at Moreton and during the journey my brother recounted the tale I have just told. The American was so thrilled to hear of someone that had actually known Lawrence that he asked if he could meet my mother. He arrived at my mother's small thatched cottage in Lulworth and spent the afternoon chatting about his "hero" and enjoying tea.

It's so sad to think that Lawrence was in so many dangerous episodes in the desert, and then came home to Dorset only to be killed in a motor cycle accident.'

'I was told a story of a couple who lived in the cottage next to the old Half Moon at Portesham. The man died and as there were no telephones in those days, his wife had to catch somebody going over to Abbotsbury to tell Mr Munday the undertaker, who would cycle over, measure you up, make your coffin and bring it back by horse and cart two days later! Somebody asked the wife where she slept as there was only one room up and one down. She replied, "In bed with my dead husband. I wasn't afraid of the old b——d when he was alive, I'm not afraid as he's dead!"'

CHURCH AND CHAPEL

At the heart of our lives was the church and the chapel, in the days when Sunday was a true day of rest and many families went to services twice a day. Children attended Sunday school, which often provided them with the only day out they had in the year and is fondly remembered.

▦ THE CHURCH AT MELBURY ABBAS ▦

'I was a church bellringer for 50 years. I joined the church choir when I was seven years old in 1906 and stayed until I was over 20. The choir had three women, five men and five boys. The rector's wife was the choir mistress and very strict. (She had nine children of her own.) If during choir practice you were spotted not singing, you were brought to the front and made to sing on your own. The rector was also a farmer and employed a man and a boy. He drove round the parish in a horse and waggonette.

The church services were long and the sermons were long. The rector bought all his sermons and didn't make up his own. They said that when they cleared out the house, there were hundreds of sermons there. On Christmas afternoon, all the Sunday school children went up to the rectory and lined up outside the front door, always taking a bag with them. They would give us sweets, apples, oranges and dates and things. Every child also had a Christmas card. It was a good thing because our parents couldn't afford to give us much. Also at Christmas the farmers would give each of their men six or seven pounds of beef. He would fatten his own stock and send them up to the butcher to be killed and dressed. Then the farmer had it back and so much was given to each man. That was our Christmas dinner.

The church was nearly full every Sunday. Nearly everybody went. You were not pressured into going. People went because I suppose it was somewhere to go and to meet up with everybody and years ago you knew everybody, not like it is today. You always had a good natter when you came outside the church. Everybody wore their Sunday best. The church was heated with hot air coming up through the floor and fuelled by burning wood and coal. It was lit by paraffin lamps. It gave you enough light to see. I think this electric light today ruins your eyesight, when you think of the wonderful needlework the women did then by candlelight and oil lamps. Not half of them wore glasses as they do today.'

▨ REST DAYS ▨

'Sundays were rest days for men and horses alike at West Lulworth. No manner of work was done on the land, save milking. The farming community, master and men, would be seen in church, the farmer arriving a few minutes late to ensure all would witness his presence.

I remember going to Belhuish Copse on Good Friday to pick primroses to decorate the church for Easter. Sunday school was a regular place to go, followed by the service. There was an annual outing to Weymouth when we were each given one shilling towards our tea. The choir outing was a trip to Bournemouth with a visit to the cinema, that was very special.'

'Sunday was a day of rest, so Gran said. Although I was baptised Church of England, we went to a Methodist Sunday school as it was

A happy Sunday school outing to Studland.

the nearest. We went at 10 am, there was a family service at 11 am, then school again at noon. When we came out we were taken for quiet walks in the afternoon on the lanes around Langton Matravers, some-times for a picnic in the summer. The Sunday school outing was to Studland sands.

Some Sundays I'd go round to Gran's, but was only allowed to read Bible stories – knitting, sewing, playing games and cards were forbidden as it was Sunday.'

▣ PORTESHAM CHAPEL ▣

'In the years before the First World War, my family all attended the Methodist chapel at Portesham twice every Sunday. My grandfather was also a lay preacher and in the early days my father was sometimes taken with him. They went by horse and trap to preach at morning service in one village, then dinner with one of the church members, afternoon service in another village, tea with someone else, then evening service in yet another village. Sometimes it was the Bride Valley or Maiden Newton area, or Weymouth. At home my aunts and mother gave dinner to the preacher who visited Portesham, and this went on until just before the Second World War.

Right up until the war, only essential work was done on a Sunday – no gardening, sewing or knitting. Granny would only allow the Bible or the *Christian Herald* on a Sunday, but my parents always had a Sunday paper, which annoyed her. The war changed country Sundays, it being necessary to do the work when the weather was suitable.'

▣ Sunday School at Abbotsbury ▣

'We went to Sunday school in the morning and then to church, Sunday school again in the afternoon and church in the evening. We were also in the church choir. I remember once my brother and his pal were sent home from church because they were dressed in short-sleeved shirts and sleeveless pullovers. I think it put them off church for a long time.

Our Sunday school day out was the great day of the year in the 1930s. We would go to Weston super Mare, Swanage or some other seaside place by charabanc. When we arrived back in the square at Abbotsbury around 9.30 in the evening, my mother would tell my brother and I to keep quiet until we got indoors, so as not to disturb people.'

▣ Our Outing to Sandbanks ▣

'Round about the 24th May (Empire Day), before the First World War, we always had our Sunday school outing from Bournemouth. We

Litton Cheney mixed church and village choir in the 1920s.

used to go by horse-drawn, and later by motorised, charabanc to Sandbanks. Sandbanks was absolutely wild in those days, not a building in sight, and we would go cockling when the tide was out in Poole harbour. These charabancs used to line up all along the Bournemouth Gardens. Sometimes we went by train to Brockenhurst or coach to Burley. We always had a cricket match on Burley pitch, girls against boys. I used to stay in the whole innings and the boys couldn't get me out, much to their annoyance – I used to block every ball. I don't think I ever made a run.

All too often it seemed to rain on the Sunday school outings and it was always said: "Don't arrange anything on the same day as Richmond Hill Sunday school outing as it's bound to rain".'

▧ SUNDAY BEST IN A WEST DORSET HAMLET ▧

'On Sundays in the 1920s we would be dressed in our best clothes and sent to Sunday school at the nearby village, which was about a mile away. We always walked there although I was only about five years old. Sometimes we had a ride back home in a car driven by a lady who lived near us. We felt very grand sitting in the dicky seat, flying along the road, home to the delicious smell of Sunday lunch.

Having been sent to Sunday school and church in the morning, after lunch we would be sent off to chapel for the afternoon service. Then in the evening in summer we would once again don our good clothes, Father would wear his best suit and hat and we would all go out for a long walk, where we would meet other people doing the same thing. This was a way of socialising, I suppose! Sometimes we would go into someone's house for a cup of tea or a look around the garden, when the men would discuss the progress of their various crops. Then it would be home to bed. We would undress in front of the warm fire and put on our night clothes, which were pretty flannelette nighties and warm hand-knitted bedsocks. We were given a candle in a candle-stick and then as my mother used to say, "Now up the wooden stairs to Bedfordshire".

We always had a Sunday school outing in the summer, which consisted of tea and lemonade on the vicarage lawn, followed by a trip to Hamberts Castle Hill, where we played rounders and picked berries and heather, then back to the vicarage to finish off the lemonade and cake. We would then walk back home, how we enjoyed it and how different from the school trips abroad today.'

GETTING ABOUT

Generations of Dorset folk relied on horse power to get them about, from the pony and trap to the carrier's cart. Bicycles, buses, trams and trains have all contributed to our memories of travel around the county.

▣ TRAVELLING ABOUT FROM WESTBOURNE ▣

'I was born in Westbourne in 1912, close to what was then called "County Gates", being the border of Hampshire and Dorset. My mother would walk over with me to a lovely shop called Brydens. They were high class grocers, wine merchants and had a large delicatessen, where they carved York ham (on the bone of course) from a china plinth, then an assistant would make up as many sandwiches as required.

Some days we would board a tram to Bournemouth Gardens and walk through to the sands where we joined my two older brothers, who had walked ahead with our folding bell tent. We used the tent for changing before a swim, and shade from the sun.

Another memory is of Sandbanks, where my mother rented a bungalow in the summer for us. There was an enterprising lady known as Miss Foote who ran a large ancient taxi in which we travelled back and forth to school. She later bred racehorses quite successfully.

To get over to Shell Bay one went by Harveys motor boat, sixpence adults, threepence children! There was of course, no road to Swanage, it was all very wild and lovely.

The Haven Hotel has (it seems to me) always been there, but along Shore Road and Haven Road was barely a house to be seen, just the odd summer bungalow in Panorama Road. When I look at it today it doesn't seem possible.'

❖ VERY LITTLE TRAFFIC ❖

'We used to come to a Dorset cottage for holidays, in about 1912. There were no footpaths in the village and very little traffic, occasionally horse-drawn vehicles or a donkey cart. There were no buses so one reached the village by train to Christchurch and there hired a trap or else one cycled. It is now a very busy road.'

Early motorbikes were on the roads before the First World War.

◼ By Carrier ◼

'As in most of England, transport at Sutton Poyntz was by carrier's van. A waggon, with a cover over it similar to those one sees in Wild West films, went into Weymouth three miles away taking an hour or so for the journey. The cottage women collected washing from boarding houses and private houses in Weymouth which they duly washed during the week by hand. On Friday or Saturday this clean washing was taken back by the same means. I think the fare was 2d. My own family rejoiced in the ownership of a pony and trap which people sometimes hired for a shilling to get to the railway station. Later, in the 1920s there was a small private bus and I travelled by this when I went to the grammar school.

It was a common sight to see a flock of sheep being driven leisurely along the lanes sometimes to market. Also a farmer would drive his cows on the road from field to cowshed for milking. No cars to be kept waiting in those days.'

◼ Travelling between the Wars ◼

'Travelling to Dorchester these days, in the comfort of the car or bus, I often wonder what it must have been like 90 to 100 years ago. My grandfather was the village carrier, or "tranter", driving his horse-drawn van from Lulworth to Dorchester on Wednesdays and Saturdays. They left the village at 7 am, arriving at Dorchester at about 10 am, returning home at 3 pm to arrive in Lulworth at about 6 pm. The fare was one shilling and parcels were also collected and delivered for sixpence. He also went to Wareham on Thursdays for the market and one morning going up West Hill the horses suddenly stopped and refused to go on. The reason was a travelling show man leading a bear on a chain had appeared. Grandad had to give the man some money to take the bear into a field before the horses would move.

Coal used to be brought into Lulworth Cove by barges, unloaded and stored in the building that is now the Beach Cafe. The bargemen

Travelling by pony and trap at Woodville Stour Provost in the 1920s.

used to bring items of blue and white pottery to sell, to earn themselves extra money. For many years the old fisherman's cottage had a dresser with this pottery displayed.

With the arrival of motor transport, buses gradually took over going to Wool and Dorchester. The first car that arrived in the village, owned by a Mr Nettleton, caused a sensation by having to go up the hills out of the village backwards!'

'In the 1920s the main transport in Alderholt village was pony and trap, horseback or bicycle. There was a bus known as the Sunflower run by Mr Ted Saunders. He also ran coach trips – one to Tidworth Tattoo was a favourite. The chances of getting there on time and getting home the same night were slim indeed!

A lorry owned by George Hood was used to transport Alderholt Band around the area for carol playing. In those days it was usual to see tyres with no inner tube but stuffed with straw. This same lorry travelled to Ringwood market on Wednesdays – he took eggs and small livestock to market for local people.

There was a railway station – very useful to go to Salisbury and all stations to Bournemouth. Unfortunately it was closed down in 1964. Its name was changed from Alderholt to Daggons Road after soldiers hoping to get to Aldershot were taken to Alderholt! – so the story goes.'

▦ EARLY BUSES ▦

'An aunt, uncle and cousin who lived in Swanage owned a car, so we visited many places not reachable by public transport. It was a real treat to go out in a car in the 1920s and 1930s. The first bus into Swanage was at 10.05 am, then every hour until 7.05 pm. The fare from Studland to Swanage was tenpence return, the bus manned by driver and conductor. We approached our bus stop via a steep hill, where one could see the road where the bus ran quite clearly, so imagine the frustration, having got up the steep hill but with the steep curve yet to negotiate, of seeing the bus pass along the top. Our kind drivers or conductors *always* looked down the hill, and if they saw someone struggling would stop the bus and wait, with a helping hand for the breathless passenger. The same drivers and conductors operated this route from Swanage to Bournemouth for years, they knew us all, great chaps!

The service to Bournemouth West station was most convenient as all Southern trains left from Bournemouth West station, straight through to Waterloo.'

'In the 1940s we used to go to Dorchester by Fred Pitcher's bus which ran on Wednesday and Saturday. It took a good two hours from Litton Cheney as he went through all the villages, where he picked up shopping lists and then dropped the goods off on the way back. He once bought a hat for a lady to wear to a wedding, and on another occasion somehow lost a carpet that had been on the bus roof.'

◙ CHARABANC AND WAGGON ◙

'In 1922, in the remote country villages, the horse and especially Shanks's mare provided the chief means of locomotion, though the invention of the internal combustion engine was fast altering the means of transport. During the 40 years of my membership of Lydlinch Women's Institute, I nearly always walked to the afternoon meetings, a distance of about two miles, by the road if wet but across Stock Park and Lydlinch Common, which was somewhat shorter, if dry. I have been known to arrive by courtesy of the drivers, in a brewer's dray drawn by two horses, in a snow-plough and in an American jeep. As I alighted from the latter, a small boy said reprovingly, "You aren't allowed to ride in an army vehicle"!

In the very early days of our Institute life, if a member wished to

attend a meeting in Dorchester, we had to travel by a motor-bus which ran from Marnhull to Dorchester driven by a Mr Lugg who had been a London bus driver. If the interior got too crowded, one could climb up a ladder onto the roof and sit on a crate of hens, surrounded by boxes of vegetables and eggs, and piles of dead rabbits, all going to Dorchester market. At one spot on the journey, I remember we were warned to duck our heads if on the roof, to avoid being struck by an overhanging branch.

When we drew up our first programme it was decided that we must have an annual outing, which drew forth the remark from Mrs "Curly" Brown (so nicknamed among ourselves, though not to her face, because she had long ringlets hanging to her shoulders), "I have all my life wanted to travel and now it is going to be possible through the Women's Institute."

In the early years we hired a motor charabanc with Cape cart hood owned by Mr Knight of the Drum and Monkey Inn at Hazelbury Bryan; he was succeeded by his son Lester, who drove us in his motor coach "Excelsior"; and latterly we were sometimes driven by Mrs Lester Knight, so members of the Knight family were our charioteers up-a-long and down-a-long for the whole of the 50 years.

One day we stuck halfway up Chideock Hill when on an outing to the west, on the very steepest incline of that very steep hill. Whilst Mr Knight standing up trod firmly on the brake, we scared passengers scrambled out and the coach thus lightened, reached the top, followed on foot by its precious load, panting heavily.

It must have been in the very early days when Mrs "Curly" Brown was still with us that we stopped in the Market Place at Chard as she didn't feel well. Our resourceful Hon Secretary, Miss Florence Cross, who incidentally was the founder of Lydlinch Women's Institute, at once produced a flask of brandy which she always carried on our outings in case of emergency. Mrs "Curly" Brown partaking of it gratefully said, "Shame to bring the good stuff all this way and not enjoy it."

The Second World War broke out and there was no petrol for joy riding; nothing daunted, we fell back upon our old friend the horse.

We proposed to picnic on a slope at Bulbarrow above Woolland House. The empty stables were prepared for our horses even down to the polishing of the brass pillar chains. We climbed up the steep hill on foot till we found a suitable picnic spot.

The following year we proposed to have a picnic again but this time on the slopes of Shillingstone Hill. As our waggons slowly approached Shillingstone the sky grew black as ink and the members anxiously asked, "What do we do if it rains?" The poor president had to reply, "I don't know!" It rained, but in the end a kind farmer allowed us to picnic in a barn where a member got oil on her dress from sitting on some agricultural machinery and another put her foot in a stray hen's nest. The storm cleared. As the horses slowly plodded homewards and we sat with our feet in wet straw on the beds of the waggons, a member was heard to remark, "This is the last time I go for an outing by waggon".'

▨ THE OLD TRAMS ▨

'I can remember when they wanted to run trams on Sundays in Bournemouth, at about the time of the First World War. The very influential members of our church, Richmond Hill, soon put a stop to that.

The conductors on the old trams used to call out at the Cemetery Junction stop: "Any more for the Cemetery?", much to the amusement of the passengers.'

Villagers from Woodville Stour Provost gathered for an outing by coach.

◈ WE HAD A RAILWAY ◈

'From my childhood days before 1939, the great difference in the village of West Moors is that we then had a railway. We could go direct to Bournemouth, Salisbury or Brockenhurst where we could change for London, or Lymington for the Isle of Wight ferry.

I lived just across the road from the railway, in a house surrounded on three sides by a builder's merchants, then called Harry Brewer and Son (my grandfather), now known as Blanchard and Burgess. Most heavy goods such as cement and plaster were delivered by rail. The storage sheds nearest the railway line were raised on brick pillars level with the platform where the goods trucks were unloaded by hand.

Through the wire at the top of the yard, I used to watch the goods trains shunting. We had a very prolific Bramley apple tree and my mother would put some apples in a bag and either the driver or the fireman would leave the train and come over to the wire to take them from me. They were always very pleased and would tell me which day they were coming back again!

I was often given a ride on the railway bogie by a Mr Baker and Bill when they went up and down the line to maintain the points etc. As you can imagine I thought this was great fun.

Most village children loved to stand on the railway bridge when a train was coming in just to get covered in steam! Also we teased Mr Wilkins in the signal box so that he would chase us with the long stick with a hook on the end which was used for lighting the gas lamps at both ends of the bridge.

On Tuesday farm animals would be sent by rail to Wimborne station which was very close to the market.'

⌗ A GREAT THRILL ⌗

'At the end of the Second World War, I was eight years old and my brother and cousin two and a half years younger. My parents somehow saved £8 and bought a little old Ford Eight, which had been laid up for "the duration" and was in *very* bad condition. Dad very carefully dismantled it and lovingly restored it, where necessary making new parts himself while Mum, on a Singer machine old enough for a shuttle, stitched leatherette squabs and fawn flannelette roof linings.

The day came that the reassembled engine was ready to run. Dad must have tried it first himself but my memory is of the great thrill, when we three children were called from play to be wedged in the back seat, holding tight, and "dared" to moved while he drove us half a mile up the Blandford Road from a bit above Hamworthy railway arches to Upton Cross and back again – without *any* doors!'

House&Home

THE WAY WE LIVED THEN

Far from the idyllic picture of rural life, with roses round the door, our homes were for the most part labour intensive, cold and draughty, no matter how picturesque. Yet we can look back on a harder way of life with some nostalgia, as it brought us such satisfaction and pleasure. This was the way we all lived then!

▣ GREAT AUNT POLLY ▣

'I was born in London but now live in Swanage. I used to visit my Great Aunt Polly in the 1920s. She died about 1930 when she was over 80.

Before I met her I was told by my father that she used to live in a thatched cottage which stood on a green in the middle of the road at Darby's Corner. Her rent for the cottage was 1s *per annum* and she was given 2s 6d each year to cover the cost of lime washing the cottage! I have an old photo of the building, though I never saw it as it was demolished for road widening.

After this she moved to a disused inn at the hamlet of Waterloo in the Cranborne Chase. For this her rent was 2s 6d per week, but she was allowed to sub-let her rooms. This was where I visited her. My family were all keen cyclists, and we would cycle down from southeast London – a marvellous ride over the North and South Downs when cycling was a pleasure – to stay with Aunt Polly. Right up to the end of her life she dug and cultivated her garden, growing all her own vegetables and fruit. She had a medlar tree and every year would send a parcel of the revolting looking fruit to my father who devoured them with delight. I refused to try them. Aunt Polly had a large cat which she would take for a walk on a lead, because, she said, he was a poacher!

Even in midsummer, my aunt wore several petticoats, including a red flannel one, and ankle length "drawers". I discovered these intimate details when I was about 16 and had cycled down from London ahead of my family to spring clean the old house and air the beds in preparation for the family's arrival, and I had to share my aunt's bed.

Another of her eccentricities was that she always put on her hat when she answered the door so that she was "just going out" if she didn't wish to ask the caller in. Of course, if it was a welcome friend, she had "just got in".

These are the lasting memories of my ancient great aunt, although I have many delightful impressions of cycling through beautiful countryside, calling on friends at Lytchett Minster, visiting Wimborne Minster, going through Wareham and on to Swanage to "Go round the World" for a penny, and down Tilly Whim Caves for threepence carrying hurricane lamps. I also remember my father's instruction to me when I first cycled to my Aunt Polly on my own: "After Romsey, straight on to Poole, turn right there and turn left at Wimborne". Those were the days!'

◙ LIFE NEAR SHAFTESBURY ◙

'Mother was widowed in 1936 at the age of 33 after only four years of marriage and shortly before I was born (I was the only child). She was born and brought up near Shaftesbury (one of eleven children) but had moved away when she left school. We returned to the Shaftesbury area in 1940 to be near my grandmother. Widowed mothers' allowance in those days was 15 shillings a week. Out of this my mother paid 6s 6d per week rent for a small semi-detached cottage which consisted of one living room, two tiny bedrooms and a lean-to lobby where Mum did the washing. There was no gas or electricity, our water came from a standpipe outside the lean-to and there was the usual bucket privy in the garden. The living room had a north facing window and a flagstone floor so it was often cold and damp. There was an open fire with an oven attached but as the flues were broken the oven didn't cook very well. Mother usually cooked on a three-burner oil stove to which a tin oven was added for baking. We had an oil lamp and candles or a torch to light us to bed.

Mr and Mrs Macy outside Court Cottage, Litton Cheney.

In 1946 electricity was installed, a light in each room but no power points. We acquired a secondhand radio and an electric iron but as there was no power point these were run from a two-way light socket! Oh, the joy of listening to *Children's Hour* on the radio. My grandmother had a wireless with an accumulator which we had to take to be recharged every week but we had never had one before. The electric iron made life a lot easier for Mother as previously she had used flat irons heated over the open fire. In 1947 a lean-to kitchen was built onto the back of the cottage with, luxury of luxuries, a sink and draining board, but still only a cold water tap! We had an electric boiler for the washing (the new kitchen boasted a power point) and this was used to heat water for our baths. A zinc "bungalow" bath was brought into the kitchen from where it hung on the wall outside. It was filled from the boiler which was quite easy as it had a tap at the bottom which went over the edge of the bath. Emptying it was a different matter, the water had to be baled out with bowls and poured down the sink.

Mother was an excellent seamstress and knitter. She made most of our clothes and often did alterations for neighbours and friends. The garden provided us with vegetables and fruit and Mother made lovely jam. Making ends meet must have been a constant battle for her. I remember her once telling me that she often had to make do with half a pint of milk a day because she couldn't afford to buy a pint. In spite of this and wartime rationing we never went hungry and I always had a Christmas stocking and a present from her.'

St Quintin's Farm, Ibberton

'In January 1940, my husband and I took over the tenancy of St Quintin's Farm, Ibberton.

The farmhouse stood in the centre of 100 acres of good old Dorset clay. There were five footpaths, one running to each of the five surrounding villages. This was good during the summer, but when the winter came it was a different story, as none of these footpaths was hard enough to take a horse and cart without sinking up to the axles in clay; so through the winter months, we were completely isolated. The children crossed the fields to and from school avoiding the paths, and when the river Divelish was in flood, they went to school on horseback!

The house was lit by candles and paraffin lamps. Cooking was done on a very large temperamental range set in a huge fireplace, with a bread oven on one side, and a very wide chimney down which the rain would pour, making the fire useless on wet days! During the nights when enemy bombers swarmed over Bulbarrow we could sit on the seats in the chimney corner and watch the fighting overhead.

The nearest drinking water was from a tap in the wood. The telephone was two miles away, and isolated places, of which there were many, had not yet been connected to electricity. Consequently, the water for baths and dairy was heated in a large boiler situated in the back kitchen, which was fired on wood and rubbish.

The toilet arrangements were very primitive – a bucket in a shed at the top of the garden path. During one very hard winter the bucket froze, and the ground was too hard to dig a trench, so until the thaw set in we were obliged to "perform" in the nearby wood! Very embarrassing, we thought, until we learned that some of our neighbours were in the same predicament! The *weekly* bath was taken in a large tin tub, and I was lucky enough to have a very large kitchen sink in which the little ones had their daily dip. For this, the water was heated in a two gallon kettle hanging on a chain in the back kitchen. During the winter, the washing was dried in the back "linney", and aired on a large fire guard. Different sized irons were heated on a grid in front of a coal fire or primus stove, which were cleaner than other fuels.

After the war, we were able to connect the house and dairy to mains water, and to run the water heating and the cooking on Calor gas. The house and cowshed were lit by Aladdin lamps.

It was a hard life, but when the summer came, and the woods were filled with birdsong and nightingales, it was a lovely place to live. We later moved with our six children to a new house with all mod cons near the main road, and life became much easier.'

▣ Life on a Farm near Wimborne ▣

'I was eight years old when we moved from the town to live on a farm in the country, seven months before the war ended. My two elder sisters and I thought it was great fun in this very old farmhouse, with no electricity, only oil lamps or candles, and big blazing log fires in the winter. We realize now what hard work it was for Mum to cook, clean and wash, and such a contrast from town life. A previous owner, whom the farm had been named after, left behind the legend that when he died, he was so enormous that the wall had to be knocked down to get him out of the house. A story we loved to believe.

One clear contrast was that in the town we very often were put to bed in the air raid shelter, where the whole family and some neighbours often spent the night. In the country we didn't even have an air raid shelter, and as children were oblivious that there was still a war happening.

After the war, we had three German prisoners of war to live in, and my father converted the huge loft above the dairy for them to share. They had their own wooden staircase to it, but it was all under the house roof. By now we had electricity, and my mother's parents and maiden sister had come to live with us as well, so we were eleven in family plus the daily workers to feed.

On reflection it was very happy childhood, and we were fortunate to have family at home whenever we came in from play or school.

The man from Dorset County Stores came out from Wimborne on a Tuesday to collect Mum's grocery order which was then delivered on the Friday.

Being a business we had a telephone, which was one of those tall ones with a separate ear piece that rested on a hook at the side, and of course, the personal operator at the exchange. I will always remember that the vet's phone number was Wimborne 1.

The house had a double privy up the garden, and just outside the back door was the old bathroom in a lean-to. When people finished their bath, the plug was pulled out and the water ran down the floor to a drain in the corner. Luckily for us, Dad installed a modern bathroom by dividing off a big bedroom: but I also remember that my eldest sister had to stand in a "cupboard" and keep pushing a button, to work an electric motor to pump water into the tank.'

▨ SWILLETTS FARM, BROADWINDSOR ▨

'When I was a little girl at Swilletts Farm, Broadwindsor in the 1930s, I remember bathing in front of the kitchen fire on Saturday nights. The water was put in a tin bath, having been heated in the copper in the back kitchen and gradually topped up. We two children went first, followed by Mum and then maybe Dad.

Toilet arrangements meant a walk up the garden path to a square building at the end of the garden. Inside was a higher seat and a lower seat, both with a hole in and a wooden lid which fitted over the hole when not in use. The whole building backed out onto the orchard and I guess someone had to clean it out by hand sometimes.

Water was all pumped up from a well which was under the front garden and was not always adequate for the needs of the house. During about the mid 1930s a pumping farm was installed in the stream in the valley about two fields away. This forced the water up to a tank on the hill in front of the house from where it would run down to supply a tap in the house and one in the cow stall. At around the same time a bath and flush toilet were installed in what had been the old cheese room upstairs, on the same floor as the bedrooms.

Although there was only a cold water tap over the bath and all hot water still had to be carried upstairs from the backhouse copper this seemed a real luxury. Hot water was not laid on until after the war and the electricity came to the farm.

A general routine seemed to be the order of the day. Monday was washday and provided the clothes were dry, Tuesday was ironing with an old flat iron. Wednesday or Thursday maybe to town one day, clean bedrooms the other. Friday was baking day and Saturday scrub flagstone floors and clean up ready for Sunday. Sunday was usually church.'

◈ VILLAGE LIFE ◈

'We had an elderly lady living next door to us at Abbotsbury in the 1920s, and every morning my mother took her in her first cup of tea and made sure she was all right. We always had her in with us for Sunday. Village life in those days was so different, everyone knew their neighbours. You could go out and leave your doors unlocked and know that everything would be all right when you got home. People helped one another.'

◈ NEVER IDLE HANDS ◈

'In the winter evenings I used to knit and sew; I enjoyed very much knitting socks and gloves on four needles. During the war we used to unravel the toes of socks and reknit them and, of course, socks were darned using a wooden mushroom to help keep the work taut.

My mother was a very skilful needlewoman and once completely reversed a coat for me, it was just like new. We also had some panels of parachute silk given to us, which was boiled to give it a golden colour instead of the dark green. From this we made some very pretty blouses, while a coloured blanket was made into a cape.

We were taught basic sewing at school and if for any reason we had to wait for help from the teacher we had to knit. No time for idle hands!'

▨ ALMSHOUSES IN MILTON ABBAS ▨

'In the 1930s I used to spend my summer holidays with my grand-mother in Milton Abbas. She lived in one of the almshouses. She had only one large room so I had to sleep in a double bed with her. Cooking and everything was done in this room and it was very crowded with her bits and pieces. The toilet was outside in a shed, with a wooden seat and spiders. Water had to be fetched from the village pump – there were only two in the long street, one near the top and the other near the bottom.

On Wednesday the bus came to take people to Dorchester market, and on Thursday to Blandford.'

▨ HOMES IN STUDLAND ▨

'Homes in Studland village consisted of mostly thatched cottages, with twelve houses built in two blocks of six in 1914 at a cost of

A peaceful scene at Studland in the days of the horse and cart.

64

approximately £100 each including land, and six houses, semi-detached, built in 1929/30 all owned by the Wareham and Purbeck District Council and built for local people's housing needs. This situation remained the same until the cessation of hostilities in late 1945 when a greater number of properties were erected by the W&PDC.

Large properties in the village included Manor House, Harry Warren House, Studland Bay House, the rectory and many more. Studland before the 1914–18 war was greatly favoured by the aristocracy, they enjoyed the sheer beauty of the village, its location and seclusion. Studland folk benefited as they found employment.

The thatched houses had a cold tap outside; nearby would be a brick wall, table height, with a large stone placed on top on which rested a washing bowl, used by the men (returning from their place of labour) to wash off dirt and dust from face and hands. Drinking water etc was carried indoors in large specially designed water cans. Wooden washstands consisted of wash basin, jug, shaving mug, toothbrush holder, soapdish and two chamber pots, and a large pail for waste water. Hot water was taken to bedrooms in large brown pitchers or cans. These essential pieces of furniture were in many village homes until well into the 1960s when mains water and sewerage were installed in the village!'

WATER, HEAT AND LIGHT

With no mod cons, we had to fetch every drop of water from the spring or well, light our homes with oil and candles, and visit the little house at the bottom of the garden when necessary!

▨ NOT A DROP TO DRINK ▨

'Water, water everywhere and not a drop to drink until we'd boiled it. I'm now 87 years old and until I moved to a flat nearly two years ago, fetching water and heating water made life very hard at times, and outdoor toilets right at the bottom of the gardens weren't pleasant, I can tell you. In one cottage I lived in since marriage we had to run across the road and up the garden steps to the toilet. Luckily there weren't so many cars on the road then. It was whilst living in this cottage that we had to cross to the other side of the road to get over a stile, walk halfway across a field, get over another stile and dip our water from an open well. Just imagine the hard work, it was easier to collect rainwater and in winter water pouring from a spring further down the road. Another row of cottages on a farm had a standpipe outside, not so difficult in the summer but come winter time and frozen pipes we had to go into the warmer cowstall and fill our buckets! In my earlier days we lived in a cottage adjoining a mill and had water all around us, plus a flooded back room in winter. In another way-out hamlet the toilet was built over a stream, forerunner of flush toilets?'

▧ No Mod Cons ▧

'As a child and teenager I lived in a small cottage which consisted of one living room and a small scullery downstairs; upstairs were two bedrooms, one had to go through the first room to enter the second. There were no mod cons. The toilet was at the bottom of the garden, very spooky when one had to go during the cold dark nights. We had to go quite a distance to the bottom of a farmyard to a pump to collect our drinking water, which we collected in pails, quite a ritual on washdays and bathnights. We used to take it in turns, a tin bath and water boiled in kettles and saucepans on the kitchen range. I can even remember having to go across a field to collect water from the sheep wash for the washing, maybe the pump was under repair.

All the cooking was done on top of the coal range or in the oven at the side. I have never since tasted a roast dinner or caraway cake to beat the flavour of the ones my gran used to cook in her oven. We had no wash basins or kitchen sinks and no electricity, we had oil lamps and candles for lighting. In those days we didn't even have toilet rolls, the newspaper was cut in squares and hung from a rail on the toilet door, and at Christmas we used to save the soft tissue the oranges and apples were wrapped in. I was born February 1925 to give you an idea of the period of "no mod cons".'

▩ FETCHING THE WATER ▩

'My parents started the post office and general store in a wooden hut in Crossways in 1927, living in the back of the hut. They built the house in 1930, the year I was born. There was no water laid on, being obtained from a well in the garden which seemed to run dry most summers.

One of my first memories is of going in the sidecar of my Dad's motorbike to collect water from the nearest stream, known as "Pat's Castle". It was collected in large drums, probably old oil drums. Water was not laid on until just before the war.'

'We lived in a thatched cottage at Woodville Stour Provost in the 1930s. We had no water at all, only a pit in the garden which was all right for wild life! My parents walked about three quarters of a mile for well water. This was carried in churns and buckets on a home-made cart and we all helped to push. Mains water came in 1936, but only as a tap in the garden, so the weekly bath by the fire went on. The lavatory was up the end of the garden (a bucket with spiders for company).'

▨ It Didn't Taste the Same ▨

'I married in 1932 and lived in a small flat in a nearby inn at Cattis-tock till a rented house became vacant for which we paid five shillings a week. There was no piped water or electricity then and a deep well with a pump served three houses. The water was lovely, ice cold and refreshing and the well was never known to run dry. No doubt there were bugs in it but no health authority men ever came to test it. I was thrilled when we were connected to the water main, but tap water did not taste the same as the old wells. Electricity was also brought to the house. Previously, washing was quite hard work; water had to be pumped and heated in an old copper in the shed. When the copper wore out, we bought a primus stove for heating the water, which I was afraid would blow up, but it never did.'

▨ Water Laid On? ▨

'When I was living in a big dilapidated house in 1919, water was laid on from a large muddy pond full of eels, roach and other fish. A man pumped this water from the scullery to a series of tanks in the attic. Being a large family (six children) this took him one or two hours each morning and evening. At night twice a week a very rusty bath was not enjoyed, as only three inches of water was allowed; often the odd tadpole would come out of the tap to join the mud coloured water.

There was only one spring of water fit to drink on the outskirts of the scattered village. A pony and cart was kept specifically to pump this water into the tall milk churn, where it lasted for a week. For the village school, a strong boy would fill a large tank on wheels on a Monday morning and drag it the one and a half miles uphill to the school porch, and take it back empty on Friday afternoon.

The kitchen was always warm because the old Eagle range heated all the water and all the cooking was done on it. Coal was bought by the half ton and came in huge blocks which had to be broken up with a coal hammer. The range had to be blackleaded and polished each day. Knives had to be cleaned each day with some type of powder on a knife-board. A fire in the sitting room was not allowed to be lit before 1st October however cold it was, and ended by the 1st April.

Bricks were kept in the bottom oven and in the evening were taken out and wrapped up in odd bits of blankets and put in the bottom of the beds.'

▨ THE LILAC TREES OF CHILD OKEFORD ▨

'The cottage that went with my husband's job belonged to the Pit-rivers estate, as did most houses in the village at that time. There was no sewerage in the village, everyone had a toilet up the garden with a bucket to be emptied in a hole in the garden. It was always easy to find the toilets as most gardens seemed to have a lilac tree planted just outside.'

▨ OPENING THE WATERWORKS ▨

'The original water supply for Weymouth was from Boiling Rock below Chalbury Hill in the Coombe Valley Road. We children at Sutton Poyntz used to put our ears to the rock to hear the water gurgling. When the waterworks were opened in the village, water was piped to Weymouth and Portland, but we were still taking our water from wells. Seven members of the parish council went to Parliament to protest and as a result seven standpipes were installed to supply free water to this village and Preston. One of these is still in existence.'

'I first saw Litton Cheney on 20th July 1940 when, my mother having died in 1938, my father married Miss Nancy Legge at St Mary's church. We then spent my father's leaves and school holidays at Redway Cottage with Nancy's mother, whom I called Granny Legge.

She had been married in October 1898 at Long Bredy. Her first home was the cottage and then on the death of her parents-in-law they moved across the road to Court House. She was always up early to feed her chickens and took her maids a cup of tea to make sure they were awake. Nancy, the third daughter, was born 24th May, Empire Day. The church bells were ringing and Granny Legge's brother, riding over from Long Bredy, thought it meant the arrival of a son. Two boys followed when presumably the bells *were* rung for their arrival. In 1938 Captain Legge sold a row of five cottages for £200. When he died Court House was sold and his widow moved to Redway Cottage.

Emmy had always come in to do the washing and this she continued to do, in a large zinc bath on the kitchen table with water heated on the oil stove. This had three burners which were cleaned with the soft paper around the oranges which you could still get during the war even though there were no bananas. A portable oven fitted over two of the burners and the dishes cooked in it were delicious.

Although Redway Cottage had full plumbing, we always drank the water which ran down rocks into a small pool in the garden. It is still lovely water and people come from Bridport to collect it. Twice a week Granny Legge ran a little produce stall outside the garage or inside if wet, when people brought excess produce, eggs, rabbits etc and others came and bought them. The profit was paid into a Post Office account and went to help the war effort. She taught me how to skin rabbits.'

※ A COTTAGE AT WOOLCOMBE FARM ※

'My family lived in a cottage at Woolcombe Farm, Toller Porcorum in the 1940s, an isolated spot near Eggardon Hill. There was no water or

Redway Cottage, Litton Cheney in the 1940s, where the water ran down the rocks.

electricity at that time. Water was brought in buckets suspended from yokes from the spring some 50 yards from the house. (The spring now supplies water for the bottling of Dorchester water.) Light was supplied by paraffin lamps and candles, the lamp glasses were polished every night and the wick trimmed; a glass had to be kept in the house in case of breakage.

Cooking was done on the open fire, with an oven on the side, supplemented by a two-burner Valor oil stove. The grate was my mother's pride, blackleaded and polished every morning and the hearth whitened with a lump of chalk from the chalk pit in a nearby field. The kettle was always singing on the hob, and once a week the flue had to be cleaned around the oven; food always tasted better from that oven! Washing clothes was done in the washhouse where the copper was kept boiling with a faggot my father cut from the hazel copse (he once unknowingly brought a grass snake back in one – frightened Mother no end when it emerged). Saturday night baths were also taken there.

The toilet was outside at the back of the house with a bucket to be emptied in a trench in the garden, excellent for vegetables! We could sit on the wooden seat (which was scrubbed once a week) and admire the view up the valley! In winter we children were afraid to go out there in the dark and had to have company with the aid of a lantern.

Being the oldest I went to school in Bridport, walking across two large fields to where my bicycle was kept in a shed, and cycling to Toller to catch the train on the Maiden Newton-Bridport line. My younger brother and sister had to walk two miles across the fields to Toller.'

▣ THE OLD FARMHOUSE ▣

'The old farmhouse in the Blackmore Vale was cold, draughty and damp in those days but is now a Grade II listed building and much enhanced by central heating, electricity and mains water. We had none of these amenities. Water was pumped from the river which ran through the farm by a powerful machine called a "ram". It was then stored in a very large tank in a barn and supplied our farm and the neighbouring one with plenty of water. I cannot remember there ever being a shortage. Light was from oil lamps and candles. Heating was from wood and coal, there being a plentiful supply of wood from trees which were regularly lopped and hedges tidily cut and laid. In the kitchen was a huge open fireplace with inglenook, bread oven, and a niche in the brickwork for standing a pot of ale while one sat in the inglenook. The fire was on a raised hearth plate with oven beneath and the only time it went out was when the sweep paid his annual visit. From an iron crossbar a hook was suspended; a large black kettle hung on this and was never far off the boil.'

◼ THE TERRACE WASH-HOUSE ◼

'I was born in 1930 in the small market town of Wimborne. My father and grandfather were both painters and decorators and my mother had been a parlourmaid at a colonel's house in the village of Colehill.

In 1934 we moved to the village of Witchampton, very much a farming community with the village school belonging to the church. I was anxious to go to school as all the girls wore white aprons, but by the time I was five years old they had stopped wearing the aprons, much to my disappointment. We had moved to this area as my father only earned about £3 per week and he thought with a large garden he could grow vegetables and rear chickens for eggs. We lived in a row of cottages called Chapel Row, with a toilet at the end of the garden and a well for the whole terrace for water; no gas or electricity, lights by oil lamp and candles and heating from the kitchen range using coal and wood. At the end of the terrace was a room with five copper boilers and tables between where the women did their washing. These coppers, of course, had to be lit early morning to get hot water to boil the clothes and I clearly remember my mother cooking her Christmas puddings in the copper.'

◼ WASHDAY ◼

'I lived with my parents in the middle house of a terrace of three cottages at Cattistock in the 1930s. The day I remember is washing day.

Monday was always the day so on Sunday my father had to fetch many buckets of water from the end house whose occupants were lucky enough to have the well with its pump and trough in their garden. The boiler in the shed was filled and the prepared fire below was lit on Monday morning. The washing seemed to take all day and it was lovely to see the very white clothes blowing on the line. When finished, the water was poured down the drain outside the kitchen.'

'I can remember helping my mother with the weekly wash, always on Monday. First we had to draw the water from a well or from the water butt where the rainwater, or soft water as it was called, collected from the house roof. All water had to be carried by bucket to fill the copper in the scullery. Next the wood and coal had to be brought from the shed at the bottom of the garden to get a roaring fire going to boil the water. All small sheets, mainly white, not like the pretty colours of today, had to be boiled to get them clean. Then came the task of fishing the clothes out of the water with a wooden pole into enamel pans or galvanised baths to rinse them. The final rinsing water had blue bag put in to keep the whites white. The final and backaching part was putting all the clothes through a wringer to squeeze out most of the water. Then on to the clothes line and the satisfaction of seeing it blowing in the breeze and drying in the sun.'

▨ THE SMELL OF PARAFFIN ▨

'Going back 45 years, I can remember going on the country rounds with my father delivering accumulators and paraffin to the houses and cottages without electricity. What stands out in my mind is the smell of paraffin being burnt in these properties, and my father saying to me, "You can't deliver to that cottage, I'll do it myself because it's infested with fleas."'

▨ ELECTRICITY COMES TO SEATOWN ▨

'In 1938 it was decided that electricity should be connected in Chideock and North Chideock. Chairman of the Parish Council, farmer

Electricity came to Seatown in 1939 – just in time for the wartime blackout!

Ernie Marsh, decided that Seatown, south of Chideock, should also have the chance of using this facility.

So it was in the spring of 1939 that at last Seatown was lit up. Landlord of the Anchor Inn, Mr Root, declared that the outside light could light up Portland at the other end of the Chesil Beach!

Before the coming of electricity to the area, Aladdin lamps and oil stoves were in use. Charlie Major came out from Bridport once a fortnight to supply residents with paraffin, candles and other necessary commodities. Farmer Ernie's wife soon abandoned the oil stove and the coal range, which had to be blackleaded and the hearth whitened every day, for a smart new Jackson four-legged electric cooker. However, washing continued to be done in the copper in the washhouse outside until the family left the farm in 1953. Early on Monday mornings the copper had to be filled, the water carried by the bucketful, the fire lit underneath, and bars of washing soap cut up and added to the water. Before electricity, the flat irons were heated on the range. The laundry when finished, starched and beautifully ironed, put the housewife of today to shame.

Farmer Ernie still continued his practice of climbing the stairs to bed in the dark, until one night he slipped backwards, causing the stair door to fly back and break a picture that was behind it. Farmer Ernie was on his back covered in shattered glass. Helping him up, his son said, "Why don't you put the stair light on, Dad?" to which his father replied, "Who the hell do you think is coming down to turn it off?" He couldn't understand about the two-way switch.

Sadly, the delight of the residents at this new found luxury was rather dampened when in September 1939 the Second World War commenced and everyone had to put up blackout curtains. There are many little stories about Chideock during the 1930s. Going to Chideock now and not a cow in sight, it is hard to believe that there were 14 small farms in the parish, self sufficient and supporting many farmworkers and their families too.'

SHOPS AND CALLERS TO THE DOOR

Every village had its own shops – bakers, butchers and grocers – and many items were delivered to our doors by local tradesmen. Cooking was often on a range or even an open fire, but we still managed to produce memorable meals from that wonderfully fresh produce.

▩ SHOPPING IN 1910 ▩

'For an occasional visit to the big town, Mother used to drive my sister and me (aged five and seven) six miles from our farmhouse. The horse drew the four-seater governess cart or trap, and was stabled while we shopped. For each individual customer, butter at the Maypole was slapped, shaped and weighed by expert use of two wooden pats.

In our village shop, loose sugar was scooped out of a drawer and transferred to a paper cone for weighing. A messenger boy cycled up one day a week to collect the order for groceries, which were delivered next day.

Our larder was a north-facing room, four yards square, with a big window. Without gas or electricity, milk was kept on marble slabs, with wet cloths to create evaporation coolness. The meat safe had a door of wire mesh, allowing air circulation but excluding insects.

There was no tinned food, but jars of jam, bottled fruit and other preserves were kept on the top shelves. A big earthenware crock would hold up to 50 eggs in its liquid "waterglass".'

❖ FOOD IN SEASON ❖

'I was born and lived on a farm situated on the outskirts of a village which contained less than 100 dwellings. My parents owned the farm where they kept cows, horses, no sheep but a few pigs for the meat supply, 30 geese, 30 ducks, turkeys, guinea fowls and hens. The lighting was by oil lamps and candles and cooking by means of the open fire or an oven heated by paraffin.

Shopping was mainly by travelling salesmen – a baker three times weekly (although there was a bakery in the village), a grocer who included paraffin among his wares and would always bring out medicines when previously requested from the chemist in the nearest town, or hardware when one's kettle or saucepan needed renewing, and a butcher. Clothing, household linens, haberdashery etc were also provided by means of a travelling salesman from a shop in the town ten miles away.

We had two ponds on the farm and it was beautiful to see 60 geese and ducks enjoying swimming on the water, at times with their offspring, the ducklings and goslings. Trout and eels were in the ponds and the rushes at the pond borders were used by the moorhens to nest, also coots and mallards. It takes me back to my happy childhood – can you imagine what a wonderful thing it is to see and to have lived with everything you need around you every day and to be able to enjoy it. We grew everything we needed in the huge vegetable garden and a fruit garden as well. The fruit included rhubarb, gooseberries, plums, damsons, pears, greengages, blackcurrants, redcurrants, loganberries, Victorias, and apples (cooking and eating) in the big orchard. The vegetables we grew were peas, carrots, onions, parsnips, turnips, swedes, beetroot, broad beans, shallots, cauliflowers, cabbage and broccoli. Out in the fields we picked blackberries, sloes and crab apples which we used to make jam, chutney and jelly. We had clotted cream, milk and made our own butter, cheese and cider. We made lovely cakes and sponges with goose eggs and I can taste them now.'

▣ OPEN FIRE AND COAL STOVE ▣

'My mother cooked on an open fire and also an oil stove with an oven. We had good meals. Breakfast was usually porridge with sugar or syrup, boiled eggs, bread and home-made jam. We had quite a few rabbit pies for dinner. We kept ferrets and my brother and I would go rabbiting on a cold frosty morning. Mother kept chickens, goats, and angora rabbits for the wool. We had a large garden but Father still had a piece of allotment and we all had to help. We were happy, but it must have been hard for our mother.'

▣ THE FIREPLACE FOR COOKING ▣

'I was born at West Lulworth in 1904. My mother used the fireplace for cooking. Most of it was done in a big pot with the vegetables tied in nets. Coal was delivered from Dorchester by a traction engine for £1 a ton. We had an outside tap for water.'

▣ ABBOTSBURY COTTAGES ▣

'Most of the cottages in the village had kitchen ranges, some had ordinary open fireplaces with an oven at the side. We had a range and it rarely went out. The ashes were very often red hot in the morning, one first had to open the damper and put a few small sticks on to have a roaring fire in a few minutes. Potatoes roasted in a coal oven were perfect, nothing tasted better.

There were two ladies in the village who baked their own bread

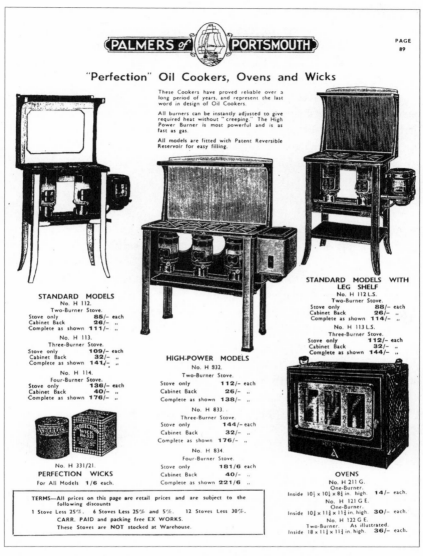

"Perfection" Oil Cookers, Ovens and Wicks

These Cookers have proved reliable over a long period of years, and represent the last word in design of Oil Cookers.

All burners can be instantly adjusted to give required heat without " creeping." The High Power Burner is most powerful and is as fast as gas.

All models are fitted with Patent Reversible Reservoir for easy filling.

STANDARD MODELS
No. H 112.
Two-Burner Stove.

Stove only	**85/-** each
Cabinet Back	**26/-** „
Complete as shown	**111/-** „

No. H 113.
Three-Burner Stove.

Stove only	**109/-** each
Cabinet Back	**32/-** „
Complete as shown	**141/-** „

No. H 114.
Four-Burner Stove.

Stove only	**136/-** each
Cabinet Back	**40/-** „
Complete as shown	**176/-** „

No. H 331/21.
PERFECTION WICKS
For All Models **1/6** each.

HIGH-POWER MODELS
No. H 832.
Two-Burner Stove.

Stove only	**112/-** each
Cabinet Back	**26/-** „
Complete as shown	**138/-** „

No. H 833.
Three-Burner Stove.

Stove only	**144/-** each
Cabinet Back	**32/-** „
Complete as shown	**176/-** „

No. H 834.
Four-Burner Stove.

Stove only	**181/6** each
Cabinet Back	**40/-** „
Complete as shown	**221/6** „

STANDARD MODELS WITH LEG SHELF
No. H 112 L.S.
Two-Burner Stove.

Stove only	**88/-** each
Cabinet Back	**26/-** „
Complete as shown	**114/-** „

No. H 113 L.S.
Three-Burner Stove.

Stove only	**112/-** each
Cabinet Back	**32/-** „
Complete as shown	**144/-** „

OVENS
No. H 211 G.
One-Burner.
Inside 10½ x 10½ x 8¼ in. high. **14/-** each.
No. H 121 G E.
One-Burner.
Inside 10½ x 11¼ x 11½ in. high. **30/-** each.
No. H 122 G E.
Two-Burner. As illustrated.
Inside 18 x 11½ x 11½ in. high. **36/-** each.

TERMS—All prices on this page are retail prices and are subject to the following discounts
1 Stove Less 25%. 6 Stoves Less 25% and 5%. 12 Stoves Less 30%.
CARR. PAID and packing free EX WORKS.
These Stoves are NOT stocked at Warehouse.

'The last word in oil cookers' – carried all along the south coast by Hampshire and Dorset suppliers.

(with coal ovens, of course). My mother's family owned one bakery and I can remember going there of an evening and seeing my great uncle and the man that worked there kneading the dough. They would start the baking in the early hours of the morning. A couple of times a week they made dough cakes and they were delicious. The village butcher used to make his own faggots and take them to the bakehouse to be roasted in big trays, the faggots covered with "flick", that was a net of fat from some part of a pig. The villagers could take their meat and potatoes to the bakehouse on a Saturday and the bakers would bake them for a penny. The butcher used to kill all his own animals in a slaughterhouse in the village.'

▨ A Jug to the Big House ▨

'In 1912, when I was ten years old, my father bought a cottage in the country for holidays. On our first visit my mother asked at the shop where she could buy milk and was told if she took a jug to the back door of the big house she could get it there. The old ladies who owned the house kept three Jersey cows and the cook used to make butter from some of the milk and sold the skimmed. One took as large a jug as one had and paid 1d. As the milk had only been hand-skimmed my mother felt it was as good as what one bought in Bournemouth for 2d a pint.

The shop in the village was above the bakery and produced extremely good bread and rolls and on Saturdays excellent dough cakes.'

▨ A Shoulder Yoke ▨

'I came to Cattistock as a young woman to teach in the village school in January 1928. I lodged in the village from Monday to Friday and went home to Weymouth for weekends.

I was surprised to see the milkman with a shoulder yoke and two pails delivering untreated milk straight from the cows. No one seemed to suffer any ill effects from this milk.

There were shops: two grocers, two bakers, a draper, a post office, a cobbler, a blacksmith, and for a time, a fishmonger. The first present my sweetheart gave to me was a pair of leather fur-lined gloves which I greatly appreciated as I suffered from chilblains. Village children gathered at the forge looking at the smiths working and listening to the grown up talk. The young ones could all swear when provoked.'

⊠ CALLERS AT THE DOOR ⊠

'The baker came to our farmhouse at Portesham once a week and on two other days bread was left in a trunk at the end of the track. It was my job to pick it up on the way home from school. The butcher called on Friday. Once a month Miss Banter called, she worked as an outrider for a firm of drapers in Bridport. All her prices finished in three farthings, but you never got a farthing change, always a sheet of pins instead.'

'The milkman came with a horse and cart, and wearing a yoke holding his churns of milk he measured a pint straight into Mother's enamel jug. Our baker at Langton Matravers came around the village with hot bread baked in a wood faggot oven. On Good Friday hot cross buns were always delivered hot by 8.30 am. The butcher came Friday with orders and to take orders for the following Friday. Eric Combes was another salesman in the 1930s. He sold anything and everything – pins, cotton, buttons, elastic, ribbons, babies' bottles, dummies, teats etc, it was amazing how he made a living out of it.'

'We sold milk at the dairy at Leigh and also delivered some, in milk cans. The baker, Mr England and later Grandad Fudge called every day. On Good Friday we had hot cross buns straight from the oven at 6.30 in the morning, the baker having worked all morning to give this service. Two butchers came from Sherborne twice a week. Tuesday you took your plate out to the van to choose what you wanted, Friday it was only ordered meat. There once was a butcher in the village, Mr Bill Willis; he lived at Cromwell Cottage and his slaughterhouse was at the back, but I don't remember that.

On Saturday a man called, he was always referred to as the "bit man", he sold paraffin, crockery and buckets, a sort of hardware store. We bought paraffin for the lamps and cooking on a three-burner Valor stove; it had an oven on two burners and a kettle on the other. The kettle held about a gallon of water and it always seemed to be boiling. A fishmonger came once a week. Mr Purden was a shoemaker, he lived at Guyers. The shopkeeper Mr Moore cut the cheese and butter from big blocks, biscuits were sold loose. There were two cheesemakers, Mr Denning of Church Farm and Mrs Matthews at Lower Totnole.'

▨ A Different Way of Life ▨

'Dorset in the early 1920s – a different slower way of life, even in a built-up area. Houses and roads lit by gaslight; indoors the lamp brackets fixed to the wall, with a chain "pull" to raise or lower the flame lit by a taper or spill. Outside the lamp man would ride his bicycle each evening, with a long pole and hook to catch the pull and light the lamps, and, I believe, extinguish them again each morning. Electricity, when it came, was wonderful and fascinating just to flip a switch, but one missed the lamp man and others like him.

Among the others were the muffin man, with his handbell and cheerful cry; the rag and bone man with loaded cart; and the milkman with his horse and cart, milk churns and bright shining brass pint and half pint measures to pour into your own jug – bottles came later! Not forgetting a piece of apple or carrot for the horse. Other remembered people were the barrel-organ man with his mournful little monkey in his bright red coat huddled on the top; the onion man from Brittany on his bicycle, strings of onions on his handlebars and carrier; the Walls Stop Me and Buy One ice cream tricycle; the knife grinder; and not forgetting the many errand boys and telegram boys. In those days a letter posted before 10 am was delivered locally at 4 pm the same day – whither progress?

I remember the two little family shops in the road: "Mrs Gilbert's" selling all the everyday needs from blacklead for ranges and bars of Sunlight soap to sugar in bright blue bags, as much or as little as you wanted. Most important was the spending of the weekly penny on sweets – farthing by farthing to get the most for your money. The other shop sold stationery and newspapers and magazines, including *Tiger Tim's* weekly if you were good.

Recreation and exercise was walking in the park, bowling a hoop, riding a scooter or sailing a boat on the lake, and looking for birds' nests in the garden hedges on the way. Church on Sundays and going out to tea meant coat, hat and gloves, winter or summer, and in school term time woe betide you if a prefect or teacher saw you walking more than two abreast on the pavement or your hat or cap not on straight – 50 lines next day!

Saturday saw the visit to the many shops in the village for the weekly shop – the butchers, bakers (not a sliced loaf in sight), grocers, greengrocers, dairy – many with a chair for the elderly or disabled to sit on while they gave their order at the counter exchanging local news. Trams ran from town to town until the buses took over. To go to the sea one walked at least one way, and if lucky caught the local charabanc back in the evening as a treat; cars were few and far between.

Entertainment at home was the "cat's whisker" wireless, full of crackles, and the wind-up gramophone with large trumpet, and games which the family played together. Times could be hard, but the streets were safe to walk and play in then.'

FROM THE CRADLE TO THE GRAVE

We were more likely to be born and to die in our own homes in the past, and both occurrences were 'village affairs' to be shared with neighbours. The doctor was called only when absolutely necessary, but unfortunately many children suffered terrible diseases such as scarlet fever and diphtheria which meant a stay in isolation. Times have changed so dramatically in the way we treat illness and hospitalisation.

'I was born at Abbotsbury in 1926. In those days it was all home births. The expectant mothers were attended by the district nurse, who was the midwife. The doctor rarely attended unless it was a difficult birth. The mothers to be in Abbotsbury were lucky as the nurse lived in the village. She was a widow by the name of Nurse Gill, who travelled to all the other villages and farms in the area on a bicycle. She had a very hard life in the winter and would always welcome a nice hot cup of tea or a hot meal.'

'All babies at West Lulworth in the 1930s were born at home and there was nothing mentioned until the actual birth. My aunt and her sister as children arrived home from the village fete to be greeted with the news, "You have a new baby brother".'

Bathing the baby in 1914 – a rare glimpse inside a cottage home.

◧ Triplets and the King's Bounty ◧

'In 1905 triplets were born to Mr and Mrs Courage at Child Okeford and an application was made for the usual King's bounty, which was an act of charity by the King to parents of triplets, if the babies lived and the parents were in poor circumstances. The couple were refused on the grounds that they were not in a position to need it. However, when the triplets were christened Mr C. J. Hunt of the Manor Farm gave the parents £3 in place of the Bounty.'

◧ Scarlet Fever ◧

'When I was eight I caught scarlet fever, a week after my sister had it. In those days patients were kept isolated until we had finished peeling, so we were in one bedroom for 13 weeks. We should have been moved to the isolation hospital which was miles over the heath. My father wrote to the health authorities to ask whether we could stay here and be nursed by our mother; as we were a little distance from the road this was allowed, but my father and brother went to stay with an uncle and aunt. As there were six years between my sister and me, I think my poor mother must have been driven to distraction, we seemed to spend most of our time quarrelling. When we were allowed out of the room, we scribbled all over the walls "Beware of the germs". The room had to be fumigated and sealed for a month, and we were taken to the bathroom and bathed in disinfectant. We were the only two in the village to catch this, so we never knew how we got it.'

'I was only eight years old in September 1935, when I suddenly got a sore throat. Nothing was thought to be wrong, but a couple or so days later, red spots appeared. The doctor was duly called, and told my mother it was scarlet fever. How I got this we don't know, one other person had it in the village, but I hadn't been to that house. I can remember a large navy blue van-type vehicle, with very small high slits as windows. I was carried out to this and taken to an isolation hospital, ten miles or so away, out on the heath near Poole. A little way off was the area for diphtheria patients. I can't remember crying, but I must have been frightened, I had never been away from my mother.

I was in isolation for six weeks. My mother and grandmother used to come and leave toys and books etc at the gate, none of these were allowed to be brought home. The ward was very spartan, high beds and very polished floors. My bed was full of dry skin, as I peeled all over. I don't remember any medicine. My brother was kept an eye on in case he caught it. I can remember my mother saying that some friends crossed over the road, when one day she was in the town shopping. When I came home, my bedroom had an awful smell and sticky paper still round the door, as men had been to fumigate and burn most of my clothes I had been wearing at the time. Today I don't hear about scarlet fever, no doubt drugs helped to banish it. There doesn't seem to be isolation for any disease, thank goodness for modern medicine.'

▣ No Visitors ▣

'When I was 13, my younger brother John and I had to be admitted to the old Boscombe Hospital to have our tonsils removed. We were in Irene Ward together with six old ladies. I remember being dressed in a white gown, and feeling giddy while I was being put to sleep with a mask over my mouth and nose. We couldn't eat at all and we weren't allowed any visitors for four days. It was considered upsetting for children to see their parents in those days. There was a box in the hospital corridor for voluntary contributions and my mother put half-a-crown in as we came out of the hospital. That was a considerable amount of money in those days.'

▣ Swanage Cottage Hospital ▣

'My appendix was removed in 1941 at Swanage cottage hospital. A surgeon from Bournemouth Royal Victoria Hospital performed the operation, and one of our local doctors, then in the RAF as a Squadron Leader gave the anaesthetic. My stay in hospital lasted just over three weeks. I was in bed all this time, apart from the last 48 hours, not even allowed to go to the toilet and bathroom. The bed was raised in the middle to keep my knees bent and body in a sitting position, then over three weeks the bed was gradually lowered to a level position! Many weeks of convalescence followed, with regular visits by the doctor. The advancement over 50 years for this type of operation is truly amazing.'

◪ BIRTH AND DEATH ◪

'My eldest sister was born at Studland in 1917, my second sister in 1920 and I was born in 1922. The family doctor lived in Swanage, journeying to the village in horse and trap and by 1922 by motor car. The doctor attended all three births, and a "maternity nurse" lived at home for six weeks to attend the mother and baby and family! The maternity nurse was experienced in childbirth and new babies, loving, and so very kind. What "official qualifications" she had, I know not, but I do know she was held in very high esteem and lovingly thought of! The maternity nurses in this case were two sisters, both married. Depending on availability one or the other took the case, they became firm friends of my parents and to us girls, to whom they were always known as "Aunty". They attended our weddings and loved our children and we in turn loved them always!

Later our area had three district nurses, two with cycles and one an Austin Seven, highly regarded by all. They attended patients in their own homes from the old to the young and the newborn, bandaged and treated minor injuries, broken bones, ulcers etc, gave bed baths and comfort to the dying!

Babies were either born at home with the district nurse in attendance or in a nursing home; we had two maternity homes in the area before Everest was opened by the NHS. Doctor's fees when I had my first baby in October 1947 included two guineas for each home visit and eight guineas for the maternity home.

The same family doctor attended us all until about 1948, he was kind, gentle and understanding and greatly loved. A surgery was held in the village twice a week; between the wars it was held in my aunt's house. The visiting room was the waiting room, a cosy room with a blazing fire in the winter, a wonderful place to meet and hear the village gossip! The consulting room was across the hall. Of course, if the patient was too ill to attend the surgery, the doctor called (a note having been left at the surgery).

Medicine was fetched from Swanage by a local lad on his bicycle. I remember large cylinders of oxygen being delivered to my Grandad's cottage to assist his breathing during the last few months of his life, and the doctor calling almost every day, and as a nine year old listening to the adults' conversation, telling how the doctor had taken a pint of blood from my Gran to relieve her high blood pressure, and hopefully assist her heart. It was something my young mind could hardly cope with, fancy doing that to my beloved Gran! The exercise was repeated but to no avail, now the advancement is incredible for such ailments.

When an elderly smallholder in the village became seriously ill he went to live the last few weeks of his long life with his married daughter. In the last days of his life straw was placed on the road and the door knocker wrapped up in straw and cloth so that no noise should disturb his last hours on this earth. I remember looking at it all as a young child and being filled with awe, just to think that the kindly old man who always wore a smock, would never again give us a ride on his old horse and transport us up the lane, over the mud and ruts!

My great grandfather who lived in a cottage up on the top of the hill died in 1929. The custom was to toll the church bell before the funeral, tolling it for the number of years; he was in his 97th year. In school that day I listened to the church bell tolling, it seemed to go on all day. Mother fetched me and my middle sister from school at 3.30 to return to Gran and Grandad's home for a post funeral tea. I met aunts and great aunts, uncles and great uncles, mostly in mourning clothes, but none the less a happy occasion, it restored my equilibrium!

Local men were always employed as the bearers at Studland funerals, best suits were worn, black ties, black boots – boots that were really black and shining – and black bowler hats.

As a mark of respect the village shops closed for a few hours, blinds and curtains were drawn in business premises and in houses along the route of the cortege. Folk stood still, and men removed their caps as the funeral party passed. Living in a village was akin to living in one big family.

It was customary for the relatives of the deceased to attend the church services (be they church or chapel worshippers) for three Sundays after the funeral, always sitting in the front seats of the church, a message of love and sympathy conveyed to them by the Reverend himself and all the village.

An old country saying: "If a body lay over a Sunday, then without doubt two more deaths would occur in quick succession"!'

◈ A Village Affair ◈

'Until fairly recent years most people in Portesham village died at home. Families had lived in the village for generations, and there was always a relative or friend to help look after the sick, there being no residential homes or hospices in those days.

After a death the body was kept at home, either in a bedroom or in the parlour, the coffin often surrounded by flowers. There were always one or two ladies in the village who were able to perform last offices.

Sometimes the coffin was removed to the chancel in church on the evening prior to the funeral. As soon as possible after death the verger would toll the church bell, one per minute for each year of the deceased's life. Whilst the funeral took place, children were kept in school and were not allowed to play in the playground which adjoined the churchyard.

A bier was usually used to carry the body to the cemetery. The village had a very nice bier with lots of brasswork, but it had the unfortunate habit of losing a back wheel, which unscrewed if put in reverse; this caused quite a bit of embarrassment at times. The houses on the way to the cemetery had curtains drawn as a mark of respect. Most families were represented at a village funeral, in fact it was usually "a village affair".'

CHILDHOOD & SCHOOLDAYS

CHILDHOOD DAYS

Growing up in the heart of the countryside or in a seaside town, we experienced the same kind of carefree childhood. We were free to go where we pleased and despite poverty and hardship – and the duties we had to take on within the family – many of us can look back on happy and secure childhood days.

▣ BORN IN THE DAIRY HOUSE AT TOLLER FRATRUM ▣

'I was born at the outbreak of the First World War in the dairy house at Toller Fratrum and was three pounds at birth. One of my first rec- ollections was that of my father signalling to the Zeppelins flying up the valley to Toller Porcorum (known as Great Toller). He held up his cup to them with me on his shoulders, they waved a white handker- chief back.

I can also remember being taken in a horse and trap to town. There was a waterproof rug and huge umbrella when it was raining. The eggs were taken to market in a large cross-handled basket, and we would see peacocks on the road when passing through Frampton. My mother told me that she rode side-saddle and carried me in a shawl when visiting her parents or relatives, or later in a pony and trap.

My family moved to Great Toller in 1918, as my great uncle Ben had died and my mother's brother had married and was coming back to help my grandfather at Little Toller. We lived in a little cottage at the bottom of Pope's Hill for several years and then moved to the old Mill House which was much larger. I can remember seeing my grand- father (who had retired then) putting a chain on the sacks of corn (one at a time) and when my brother and I had climbed two flights of steps to see a sack bag come through the flap, we had to shout that it had done so and pull the chain to stop, then Grandfather would come up until the grain had flowed into a bin. I should have added that this took place after the harvest, late autumn. Earlier I can remember going out to see the sheaves of corn being stacked up all around the fields.

When I went to the village school I wore a white pinafore over my dark dress. Both teachers lived in the village. My cousins rode ponies to Toller school and came and had dinners with us, which my mother had cooked.'

⬛ LAST BUT ONE OF 14 CHILDREN ⬛

'I was last but one of 14 children, born in Weymouth of good parents. My father and his brother sailed on the tall ships and he told us how dreadful it was rounding Cape Horn. Later he was a diver; if any fisherman's nets got fouled he would recover them, but would take no reward so instead we often had lovely fresh fish brought on a dish to our front door. My oldest brother was on the *Titanic* and was in the rescue boat and helped Lady Duff Cooper, the next brother was on the *Lusitania* and was also saved. Another brother was in the Royal Navy and one on the Jersey boats.

We thought the big slabs of cocoa chocolate were lovely and we watched Dad cut his cucumber shape of tobacco with string all round. Simple pleasures in those days. We didn't have chairs but long stools for our meals and our eyes would watch the cane hanging on the hook in the ceiling above my mother's head. We had at that time a lovely Airedale dog who stayed under the table to partake of any food you didn't like, or you would have it at the next meal, or next day. Before breakfast we would have to run up one street and down the next with our hoops. Breakfast consisted of sixpenny worth of bacon pieces from the Civil and Military Stores, meat dishes piled with fried bread and apple slices and, if you were very lucky, you had some Nestlé's condensed milk on bread. If ever we had boiled eggs, one was shared with the white and the next time you had the yolk, hard times but very happy.

We didn't have many playthings as one of my brothers was blind through neglect at birth and while my mother was breastfeeding me she had to go off to London with him, so my father was proud of the

Children of both sexes were often dressed identically until quite a late age. This two year old boy lived at Dorchester.

fact that he weaned me with a sugar tit, which was a muslin bag filled with sugar and dipped in milk. To her surprise, when my mother returned I was in a cot and another baby in bed with Dad; she was left on our doorstep by a woman who had been paid a lump sum, while the actress mother was on tour. They said my father was broken-hearted when they traced her, he didn't want to part with it, what a glutton for punishment.

We had very few toys as every time my brother came home from the blind school at Portsmouth he would have a next size Meccano. My mother would ask us and explain we at least had a home life, so of course we all agreed. I had an old doll with no head which I dressed and loved, and put her in the cradle made out of a shoe box. My mother promised to buy me a head from Guppy's shop at Weymouth one day, but it didn't happen.

We all had our tasks to do weekly and when my father grew cabbages etc on his allotment we used to go round the houses to sell them, first having to get our 6d toll ticket from an office next to the Wesleyan church (where incidentally I had my first Sunday school book prize, *Uncle Tom's Cabin*). We used to do shopping for up to a penny, then we spent ages making our minds up at Risley's shop whether to have misshaped chocolates, sherbet dabs or liquorice bootlaces; sometimes it would be broken biscuits at Stickland grocery store. Often it would be Neal's nuts.

My mother had her treat every week to the Palladium picture house. We had orders to keep the fire going, but one night we were so busy playing ludo that it nearly went out, so my brother threw some paraffin on it. The bobbled mantlepiece cloth went first. The horror we felt when we saw my mother's slippers, just half of them left. My mother said, "Up them stairs before I come up and belt you", but I think she was thankful it wasn't worse. I had to blacklead the fire and the grate and emery cloth the fender, plus an extra shake of the rag rugs that my brothers would make on their voyages at sea, my God they were heavy. Another time we had to meet my mother's friend, Mrs Butler, from her worship next to the Co-op stores and in those days there was a deep pond behind the pub where Beets used to season their wood, so we used to ride on the wood. Imagine our horror when my brother fell in. The smell was dreadful. I took him to the church and they did what they could before we made the long trek home. Once again we were for it, but we never did get knocked about.

My father used to go out in the lifeboat at night and my mother used to walk about and pray for their safety, but with the money in the morning we used to have to go down to Dunnings in Hope Square to pay the bread bill and they gave us a bag of shop cakes which we thought was wonderful, as Mum cooked everything every day.

There were always cross-handled baskets of Tom Putt apples hanging above our heads, I don't ever see them now. At the door, which was never locked in those days, we had the paraffin man, coal man, watercress fresh from the spring, and Minnie the milk lady with her milk yokes either side of her shoulders with the gleaming dippers. The joy one day when I answered the door and the man asked for a match and he turned out to be a "Blue Cross Match man" and so my mother had a couple of pounds and because we were two under 14 years old she had 50 shillings each; a pound was a great deal of money then.

My mother used to walk the streets of Weymouth with just a whistle in her white apron as she was called to lay people out and all the old borough police knew her and she was loved and respected in Weymouth. When the Holy Trinity school was taken over by various armies we always had soldiers in and out of our house. When the Scott Regiment moved out they fitted my young brother with a lovely uniform kilt plus trews, but needless to say he wasn't so keen. My mother had a drawer full of different badges, including Australia, I wish I had them now. Our front door, as I said, was open and any sailor who missed the liberty boat would just quietly go to bed, make a brew of tea in the morning and leave the money on the table. I never heard of anyone doing a dirty trick.

The small treats that we used to look forward to would be looked at with scorn now: the joy of a big dish of frumenty at Easter with its wheat and spice; taking the sugar out of the mixed peel when mincing everything for the mincemeat at Christmas; the smell of the piccalilli cooking, the pickled onions and red cabbage, and my mother used to do some lovely mixed vegetables in vinegar, I would love to have some of them now; the lovely four-pound doughcakes of Mr Dunning, where at Christmas Mother used to order one fruit and one caraway seed and his Christmas present to us was one of each.

We made a cart (of sorts) and steered it with rope and we collected the manure from Groves the blacksmith and took turns to sit on the manure and the other steered; it was trouble if anyone got there before us. Then we would fill up with acorns to keep the copper fire going to boil the whites. In the autumn we would fill up with leaves.

I hate the smell of camphorated oil as it was kept hot on the hob and I went to school with a silk scarf round my head when suffering from swollen glands. My mother wouldn't let the doctor do anything, she called him a "horse doctor", but I have no idea why.

I was always called "Fatty Arbuckle" after the large actor, as I was fat, or Simple Simon as my initials were SS. I was not altogether happy at school.

For coppers my mother used to do an old man's change of clothing once a week for ninepence. In those days, we had three baths of water and as Mum was putting his flannels in she had to go to the front door, so, as I thought, I was being helpful and I put the pure flannel drawers in the copper. Oh, my mother went mad, they were just one mass of jelly. God knows how many weeks she had to wash to make up that money. After she cooled down, she knew I was trying to help. Oh, the hard work turning the old mangle. Then when the sheets were dry we had an old sheet tacked round the mangle which we put the sheets and towels through to save ironing and it worked well. We kids thought it was wonderful to have newspaper instead of tablecloths at dinner times Monday, as it was all in the wash.

I wonder how many children would sleep five in a bed, two up top and three down the bottom, but it kept you warm. On one wall of our bedroom were net bags full of white Windsor soap to harden to last longer, carbolic soap, onions, marrows etc.

If we had a penny ride on the old train from Rodwell station to Wyke we thought we were the cat's whiskers. From there we would walk to Chesil Beach and pick our mother some sea pinks, which she loved. Sandsfoot Castle was our main playground and many a penny we earned digging bait for the fishermen.'

◈ Growing up in Bournemouth ◈

'My life began in Bournemouth on 1st May 1915, the third daughter of a family of nine. We were all born in a six-roomed house, with a large garden that belonged to my grandfather who was a widower. My parents worked hard and gave us all a wonderful happy childhood. A nurse was in attendance at the births and my mother would have ten days in bed each time to recuperate. As we got older, we would look after the younger ones. We did not have much money, but we had plenty of fruit and vegetables to eat.

FAIRY CYCLE

No. 1 Ball-bearing Rubber Pedals. Adjustable plated handle bars with cycle grips, ⅞-in. wired-on tyre, 12 in. wheels, cone bearings, adjustable cycle saddle, brake, free-wheel, and mudguards.
PRICE **59/6**

No. 2 With ⅞-in. ribbed tangent spoke, ball-bearing wheels. PRICE **87/6**

My father had a fish round in Winton, which earned him a living. The fish came from Grimsby each day, and he collected them from Central Station with his donkey and dray, and then went on his rounds calling, "Fresh fish alive!" It always amazed me that he could spend all day selling fish to his regular customers and then at night remember all that they had had, to be entered into his book to be paid for at the end of the week. My brothers used to help him on Saturdays.

We also had a pony and trap with side seats, and at weekends, we would all get dressed up, we girls in white frocks and hats and the boys in home-made suits, and we would go off for trips around the countryside. One weekend, we did get to East Lulworth, which was where my grandfather had come from in the 1870s. It seemed a very long journey, we went via Wareham and when we got there, the farmer allowed us to sleep in his loft among the hay. We hung our silk frocks on the stacked hay, and in the morning when we woke, we looked down the ladder to see Grandad below – he was a very dear man. He used to take us to church on Sunday mornings and on passing the sweet shop on the way home, he would give us all a penny, which bought four kinds of sweets, all in different bags.

We were lucky to have plenty of space for playing. There were allotments at Talbot Woods and many fields, now sadly all built up. On Saturdays in the summer we used to help dig potatoes and other vegetables at the allotment in Roslin Road. Each child would have a sack for collecting dried grass for the chicken coops – Mum kept chickens at the top of the garden so that we had plenty of eggs and also baby chicks, to our delight. We played hopscotch, skipping, hoops, marbles and walking on our hands, showing plenty of leg!'

'I lived in one of the oldest cottages, I believe, in Bournemouth, mainly in Boscombe Grove Road. It leads off the Old Ashley Road in Boscombe. There I lived, in one of two little cottages amidst fields, if you can imagine. There were fields either side of me. On one side, a Mr Fudge kept sheep to graze in there. Well, every now and then, he would drive them up the road. Imagine, a man walking in the middle of Bournemouth with a flock of sheep up the main road to the abattoir. He also owned his own butcher's shop, and when he used to go up the road, my brother, who was considerably older than I, and like all boys, he was a bit of a bully, used to make me cry by saying the sheep were to be killed. He was quite right, of course.

One of the highlights of the year was when Mr Fudge would kindly let out his field to a fair, Coldstuds Fair, I remember. We had lots of flares, I can remember, around the coconut shy. The fairground people used the water from our house, don't ask me how they did it in those days, but they managed to have a tap at the bottom of the garden. My brother and I were allowed to go to the fair any time we liked and go on everything. As you can imagine, we made the most of this. The only thing was, we were not allowed to keep the coconuts which we managed to hit down. And then again, one more week in the year, this kindly Mr Fudge would let out the other side of the field to what was called a menagerie. In these days it would be called a mobile zoo, I presume. There were no circus acts or anything, there were just a few animals stuck behind bars. I can well remember the elephant, a lion, a tiger and a few monkeys. I was always being told, if I wasn't a good girl that week the lion would get me. I would go to bed, and I could hear these animals roar and I used to be really frightened of them.

As I can remember, our entertainment was very limited in those days. Along the beach we used to have what was known as the Billy Cave Revels and pierrots. That meant, there was a concert party staged on the actual sands itself. This was a great event of the year, it used to be there for about two months. As a matter of fact, one of my uncles was in it. We used to pay about twopence in those days to sit in the deckchair. If you didn't watch out, halfway through the performance the tide would suddenly come in and you would find your feet wet. Sometimes the chairs have been known to float out to sea.

Obviously, we didn't have the money which is available now. Also going into Bournemouth along the front, the Bournemouth Gardens weren't anything like they are now. There was a little rustic bridge and you were not, and I mean *not* allowed to go on the grass. In fact, the park-keeper would be watching you very carefully. Where the swimming baths originally were, which now have been pulled down to make way for a car park, there was a hotel called the Bellevue Hotel. I vividly remember two tubs outside with bay trees in, because the donkey invalid carts used to be there. If the donkeys weren't available to pull them, we as children were able to earn a halfpenny each, which was a lot of money, for pulling a bath chair, with someone in it, not always small either, right along the front from one pier to another. And this all for a halfpenny. A halfpenny went a long way in those days. Ten aniseed balls perhaps, if you were lucky.

We seemed to have very severe winters years ago, but also beautiful summers. In the winter I can well remember the men going with pickaxes along the railway lines hitting out the ice to make room for the trams to drive along. These men were up sometimes all night picking away getting the ice out of the rails, so the trams could drive along comfortably.

When I was nine or ten, Edward, Prince of Wales, came to Bournemouth. In those days it was quite an event to be visited by Royalty. I was very honoured to be chosen to take part in a country dance, in the formation of the Prince of Wales's feathers, in Meyrick Park in Bournemouth. For this I had an enormous sheet wrapped around me. Trying to dance with a sheet around me was a bit of an effort, but I made it. We had to do various corners and form the Prince of Wales's feathers. Lots of effort went into this, but it was well worth it. I distinctly remember walking past the Prince of Wales, who stopped and said, "Thank you very much for your beautiful dancing, I really enjoyed it." Well, as you can imagine, I was only a young schoolgirl, I was thrilled to bits. What a difference, how they used to wander around in those days, just walking along Meyrick Park. They didn't have escorts, policemen or detectives. It was just a simple matter of a manservant with them.'

▨ LIFE IN A COUNTRY HAMLET ▨

'I was born in 1925 in a hamlet in West Dorset. We lived in a small cottage. My father was a plumber, and money was not plentiful, but

It was always a delight to travel by pony and trap: Mr Harris and his grandchildren at Langton Matravers.

I can't remember that fact meaning anything to me. I was one of a family of five and my memories of those days are very clear in my mind.

We always had good food, mostly grown by my father in the cottage garden. We were taught good manners and had good books to read. I recently returned to that cottage and wondered how on earth my parents managed to exist with all of us, in so small a space.

We were all unaware that anything was amiss, in any case everyone in the country lived in exactly the same way and I think we were all much more content with so much less than today. We had no electricity, or water laid on; water had to be fetched in a bucket from a nearby well, and lighting was by oil lamp or candle. On washday it was my father's job to fetch the water and fill the copper and light the fire under it, so that the water would be ready (after we had been sent to school) for my mother to commence the weekly wash, which lasted all day. I remember we always had boiled rice for Monday's evening meal, as Mother used the rice water to make starch for the clothes.

The same two teachers remained at the school for the whole of my school life. We learned the three Rs and did a lot of play-acting and physical exercise. I hated the visit from the "Nit Nurse", who always seemed to have cold hands and pushed them down the back of your neck to pull up your vest to see if it was clean, and then combed your hair to see likewise.

In the school summer holidays ·when, of course, the sky was always blue and the sun always shone, we would go off for days in the hayfields, and help the farmer load the waggons with hay, then when the hay was unloaded onto the rick we would all climb into the waggon and ride across the field to where it had to be reloaded all over again. The farmer's wife brought tea in big hampers for the workmen and we were included and given strawberries and cream, but not the cider! The same thing happened at harvest time, but then we would walk around behind the thrashing machine and try and catch a rabbit as the poor frightened thing tried to run away. At the end of the day the farmer would share the rabbits that were caught, amongst the workers, and we children were over the moon to be going home with a stick on our shoulders with a rabbit at each end. Mother would be pleased to have something to supplement the larder.

There was a lot more charity in those days. For instance, I was sent to the farm to collect the milk in the can every evening. I often had to wait for the farmer to finish milking the cows, which he and his wife did by hand. I would be waiting and watching for them to come back to the farmhouse carrying the buckets of milk on either side of a yoke across their shoulders. They would then tip the milk into cans, strained through muslin. The farmer's wife always gave me a glass of warm milk straight from the cows before I went home and often she gave me some eggs. In the autumn time she would give me a basket and say, "Go and help yourself to some apples." Now everything has to be sold for money.

It all seemed very primitive in those days, but I am still here at 71 years old, quite fit and healthy. What else do I remember about my Dorset life? Walking in the woods picking armfuls of bluebells and primroses which we tied in bunches and sent to London to some Guides, who sold them to raise money for the poor children to come to the country. I remember an exciting day when they came and camped at Poole, and we were invited to meet them.

Another memory is of the time the road through our hamlet was tarred for the first time. The excitement of the steam roller and the smell of tar which seemed to stick to everything and to last for days.

Of sheep shearing days and sheep washing days, of days making daisy chains in the fields and playing in the rivers, catching tadpoles amidst the golden iris and kingcups and cuckoo flowers and wearing our Dorset sunbonnets, with never a thought of being abducted (what freedom we had then). Of gathering hazelnuts and chestnuts and blackberries, picking mushrooms by the basketful, flying our home-made kites and catching butterflies in nets we had made from wire and old lace curtains.

Of the long walks to the nearest town to do the weekly shop with Mother and helping her carry the heavy baskets home.

Of walking the two and a half miles to visit the doctor. Of meeting the District Nurse always around on her bicycle, constantly telling my mother, "Get that girl's fringe cut or she'll squint", but I never did.

Of the longed for day when the travelling shop came around, selling everything from cotton reels to paraffin. We were allowed a bar of pink and white nougat on that day, a big treat.

Once a year we had a trip to the seaside, how lovely that was, Mother always brought mackerel to fry for our supper when we got home. I can smell them now, all fresh from the sea with their tails turned up.

Of walking home from the school through the woods and stopping to dismantle a stile and have a see-saw, watching a man making hurdles for the sheep-pens from withy sticks in the wood. Of making whistles from sycamore bushes.

Of singing hymns with Mother by the fire on winter Sunday evenings.

Of the wonder of Christmas morning, when the house was transformed into Wonderland. The Christmas "tree" was a large holly branch, but who cared, Father Christmas had been and left an orange, a box of dates and some nuts in my stocking which had been fixed to the end of our bed by a clothes peg; it was ecstasy.'

GAMES AND SIMPLE PLEASURES

Our games followed the seasons and we usually played in the roads and lanes, untroubled by traffic. We found pleasure in simple things, as many families could ill afford luxuries and expensive toys, and even our 'crimes' now seem so innocent.

◼ THE HIGHLIGHT OF OUR YEAR ◼
'One of my most vivid childhood memories is of an annual outing with my mother and father. Dad worked at the local clay mines but he did own a little rowing boat. So, with a borrowed tent, we would set off for Redcliffe down the river Frome to Russell Quay which is situated on the north-west side of the Arne peninsula.

As we always stayed for the weekend Dad's first job was to dig a hole above the high water mark to get fresh drinking water.

On one particular occasion there was an exceptionally high tide overnight. Next morning we made our cup of tea from the clear water in the hole but found we were unable to drink it because it had filled with salt water during the night. Dad had to start digging all over again.

This weekend was the highlight of our year and Dad would spend the time fishing whilst Mum and I went for long walks through the heather.'

▣ PROUD OWNER OF A HOBBY HORSE ▣

'When I was a young child in the early 1950s, the love of my life was horses – or perhaps I should say the hobby of my life was horses, as I was the proud owner of a stableful of hobby horses. Whenever my father or elder brother outgrew a pair of socks or my mother's thick lisle stockings refused to undergo yet another visit to the invisible menders I would pounce on them and spend a happy evening stuffing them full of old rags, sewing on button eyes and wool for manes, and making a bridle from any spare bits of braid, with curtain rings for bits. With a garden cane firmly tied on, I would proudly ride out in the morning to show my best friend (and fellow hobby horse breeder!) my new stable companion. Between us we had bays, greys, chestnuts, duns, in fact most colours – except black. I suppose our fathers kept black socks for funerals so they only rarely were disposed of. (My friend did acquire a black horse one day, to my deep envy, but it turned green once it had been ridden out in the endless sunny days of our holidays.)

We had boundless freedom in those far off days and could "ride" all over the countryside around Dorchester, even over the hills into Came Park. We "hunted" regularly with our two faithful mongrel dogs as our hounds. Having the great good fortune to attend Sunninghill prep school, we sported scarlet blazers, perfect for a Master of Foxhounds and his huntsmen.

106

When we grew hot and thirsty (for hobby horses can gallop for great distances!) we would knock on a cottage door and ask politely for a glass of water. People were always happy to see us and we never thought twice about knocking on a stranger's door for we knew nothing of any of today's dangers. I remember my early childhood as a time of great freedom.'

◼ Games and Sweets ◼

'For going out in about 1919 the girls wore black laced-up boots, and the boys boots and gaiters, but most of the time we all wore galoshes.

Although we were very isolated and met few people we were always happy. In the spring much time was taken looking for birds' nests and collecting eggs, but never taking more than one from any nest, to add to our collections. The same applied to butterflies. Never more than one species was allowed in our collection. We killed them by chopping up laurel leaves, putting them in a jar and dropping the butterfly inside where it died very quickly.

We had no bicycles, just wooden scooters with wooden wheels to go the mile and a half to the post office and village shop to spend the weekly one penny. This would buy a stick of barley sugar with a piece of string through it, or two gobstoppers, four sugar mice or perhaps a tiny bag of sherbet. We all had skipping ropes and hoops. In the autumn the time was taken up catching leaves. To have twelve happy months the following year, twelve different types of leaves had to be caught.

On Sundays we all walked the two miles to church across the fields. We all had to leave the collection for one day, and were not allowed to play any ball or card games.'

◼ Little Devils ◼

'When I was growing up in Cattistock in the 1930s we had a village bobby. We respected him and we never knew when he was going to turn up on his bicycle. We weren't perfect children and my friends and I used to go up the valley to pinch turnips, wash them in grass or in the cows' trough and eat them. Apples were also on the menu from previous scrumping. Knocking on doors and running away was considered fun. We thought we were little devils, but how different from today's crimes.'

▩ A FAVOURITE PLAY AREA ▩

'On the Blandford Road between Hamworthy and Upton in the 1940s, there was far less traffic than now, even on weekdays and a lot of that was still horses. Milk came by horse and float; coal and fresh fish by horse and cart, as did the rag-and-bone man too.

Big horses and carts also brought loads of sawdust, from Rigler's timber yard on Poole quay, up our drive (our landlord was a Mr Rigler) to fill in the large ponds in the worked out clay pits behind our house. In time, plants and bushes colonized the area and, despite warnings, it became a favourite play space and the big boys' bonfire site. Round the edges, the sawdust was thinner and quaked if we walked on it and, further out, it became bog and small pools with interesting wildlife. I once had to be pulled from the sucking bog and more than once, our fathers had to help drag out struggling gypsy horses. (Their other frequent amateur rescue service was to beat out fires in the heather beyond, started by sparks from the nearby railway line.) From the heath and ponds was a small belt of trees and rhododendrons and the old orchard, all once grounds attached to the house but used as a common playground by us and the neighbourhood youngsters. Bounded by railway line and newer buildings along the main road, access was by almost secret footpaths and one narrow sandy lane. Now, I believe it is all covered by a housing estate.'

▩ GIRL GUIDES ▩

'I joined the very first Girl Guides in Bournemouth in 1918, my sister the first Brownie pack. We had marvellous Guiders, daughters of well known people in Bournemouth. Our Captain was Myfanwy Jones,

A family picnic at Freshwater Bay, before the First World War.

daughter of the great Rev Dr J. D. Jones of Richmond Hill Congregational church in the Square. Our Lieutenant was the daughter of the Food Controller of Bournemouth during the First World War. We Guides absolutely adored these leaders. It was through Miss Jones's efforts that Dudsbury Guide Camp was procured for the Guide movement. She was about to become County Commissioner when she was knocked off her bicycle by a lorry during the war, in Bournemouth Square, and killed. She was a terrific loss to Guiding. Our company was the very first to camp at Foxlease in the New Forest in about 1919 and it was because of our good behaviour that it was handed over to the Guide movement by an American lady, Mrs Archibald.'

▧ COUNTRY TREATS ▧

'My father was a carpenter and during the Second World War cycled from East Lulworth to Warmwell, about twelve miles, and back every day to earn a living to keep us, two brothers, myself and Mother. My mother was a teacher who had left school at 14 and started teaching the next term – no training, and then left to have her family. She went back to teach at Wool RC school when I went to school and she cycled there and back each day before the bus service.

There were no uniforms at my junior school at East Lulworth but everyone wore shoes, not boots, as in my mother's time. In our spare time we played in the woods nearby, hide and seek being a favourite, or marbles, skipping or hopscotch on the road, all played in due season. We were not angels, I can remember my brother saying that they were taught a lesson by a "clip round the ear" by the local policeman, when they were caught scrumping or in some other minor wrong doing.

Although living only three miles from the beach it was a treat during the summer to go to Lulworth Cove. I remember the turnstiles at the toilets at the cove – I tried to go in the out turnstile and consequently got caught by my neck and a gentleman came and took the mechanism apart to release me.

Haymaking was great fun as we were allowed to ride on the cart

from the farm back to the fields. I remember I always wanted to ride on top of the load. We used to drive the horses and later the tractors long before leaving school.

East Lulworth is on a large agricultural estate and all the houses were and still are owned by the Weld family. As a child I remember a party for all the village children was a treat at Christmas and later this was a visit to the pantomime in Bournemouth.'

'In the school holidays my brother and I had to help on the farm at Creech; sometimes we were sent out to the fields to cut ragwort and when Mum came to bring our dinner she would look around the field and if we had not done much work she would say, "I see you have had Lawrence on your back today."

I have vivid memories of butter making when I was a child about 80 years ago. The cream was put into the churn which had a spindle attached; this went through the wall and was driven by a horse walking round and round and my brother and I had to take turns to drive it, a job we hated as sometimes the butter would not come and Mum would say it had gone to sleep, and put in a drop of water. All the utensils were scalded with water from the copper and then plunged into cold. When Dad was working out the buttermilk and adding the salt, Mum would give us two big crusts of bread and Dad would put a big dollop of butter on them with his thumb.

On Oak Apple Day, if you didn't wear an oak apple to school the boys would sting you with a nettle.

Threshing was an exciting time for us children. When we heard the steam engine coming down the farm track we rushed out to see it arrive. Next day the engine driver would come very early to get up steam and when work started Mum would be busy keeping the men supplied with drinks. It was a very dusty job, sometimes we were allowed to take charge of the bags catching the dust. When the men were reaching the bottom of the rick we stood waiting with sticks, and the farm dogs, to kill the rats as they ran out. We would then lay them in a row on the low wall which ran in front of the house to be counted at the end of the day.'

▨ ONCE A YEAR ▨
'Growing up at Chedington in the 1930s, we went to Weymouth for our Sunday school outing once a year, for which we saved up all our pennies for ice creams and sixpenny necklaces from Woolworths.'

SCHOOLDAYS – THE BEST YEARS OF OUR LIVES?

Generations of Dorset schoolchildren remember long walks to school, wet clothes steaming around the stove or open fire in the classroom, small village schools that taught all ages in one room, and the cane that was so often used. Yet many of us also remember good and caring teachers who worked hard with little equipment and few amenities.

▨ SCHOOL IN 1903 AT MELBURY ABBAS ▨
'My mother was required to work in the farm house, so at the age of four in 1903 I was sent to school, where I continued until 1913. We

were taught reading, writing, arithmetic and religion. The school was run by the rector's two daughters and he came to the school often, to take morning prayers. A school inspector used to come to test us on religion and we were "polished up" on the subject before these visits.

Discipline was very strict, the boys had to put their hand to their cap to the teacher, even when outside the school. I was caned once and that was for something I didn't do. One of the boys hid a girl's hat in a drainpipe. I was blamed and was caned, with outside play stopped for six weeks. Before the time was up, it was reported that another boy had done it. The rector came to the school and gave me sixpence. The cane didn't worry me much, perhaps it was worth sixpence. The school toilets were open. There was no running water, the two biggest boys had to draw the water from the 90 foot deep well, by bucket.'

▨ WEARING PINAFORES ▨

'In 1927 I had started school at Leigh, wearing long black boots, black stockings, a navy serge dress and a white embroidery anglais pinafore. My sister started school two years later and did not wear a pinafore, so it had gone out of fashion by then.'

▨ BOURNEMOUTH SCHOOLS IN THE 1920s ▨

'Play things and pastimes for boys included marbles, spinning tops, conkers in season, and hoops. I had taken my hoop to St Luke's school one day, *only* once as it was a very big iron hoop, larger than me and during play time I was bowling it round and round on a small paved area where a teacher was sitting hoping to enjoy a quiet cup of tea. You can imagine the scene and firm request, "Don't bring that thing to school again!" – it was probably driving her crazy. I would mention also that we sat on wooden forms in class and according to my mother I came home on more than one occasion having knocked out a tooth on the form dashing into the classroom from play. Not very orderly but we were very young.

Bournemouth schoolchildren in the 1920s.

I left the infants' school when I reached five years in 1921 and attended St Walburga's Catholic school in Yelverton Road, Bournemouth town centre. It so happened that the school was within a stone's throw of where my grandparents had lived when they first came to Bournemouth. This school was about three miles from home and I walked each day with my older sisters except in extremely bad weather when we travelled by tram. I believe it was one penny return from Winton to Richmond Hill.

I would mention that the route for walking to and from school passed between allotments with vegetables grown by working people and this in my mother's day was open common ground when she walked to school. Needless to say, it was fully developed with rather nice houses in the late 1920s and 1930s. Back to the school: it was one of the large original Bournemouth houses converted for school use and two of the classrooms were extremely spacious with large open coal-burning fireplaces; very comfortable in cold winter months. Being a mixed school the boys' and girls' quite lengthy playgrounds were separated by an iron fence and the same at the bottom end of both, which fenced off a small area of trees, the fence essential as there was a considerable drop down to the Yelverton Road pavement. This was the school that my mother and her brothers and sisters and cousins attended.

It was permissible in later years to go out of school at lunch times and we boys often went to Meyrick Park to play football but only with a small tennis ball or similar, our coats as goal posts of course. Also we sometimes went to Horseshoe Common which was a natural wooded area at that time, with wildlife undisturbed. It was considered quite an achievement to know the route through the undergrowth to reach the pond hidden in the middle which contained the usual schoolboys' delights – tadpoles, small fish, frogs, etc whilst dragonflies, butterflies and wild birds flew in profusion. A visit to Russell Cotes Museum on the East Cliff was another activity and I feel I must mention that with money not being too plentiful in our large family, we got to know the town centre shops where for a penny we could buy some "pecked" fruit, sticky sweets, broken biscuits and "stale" cakes, (were they really that stale? – on reflection I feel they were being kind to us).'

'I went to Bournemouth School for Girls the day it opened in 1919 at the Lansdowne Municipal College. My Dad had to pay over £3 a term for me, a lot of money in those days. My mother had to let lodgings in the summer to visitors to help pay for my education.

After the First World War ended, on Peace Day our headmistress wouldn't let us out of the school to celebrate, when everyone else was enjoying themselves. She would never let us off on Wednesdays to go to our Sunday school outings as she said they were only for *slum* children and she wouldn't let us play netball or hockey matches against other schools, only if they were posh private ones.

One episode I can remember very plainly while I was still at school. An aeroplane came very low over Derby Road, hitting the overhead tram wires and crashing in flames just where Bowmakers stands today, and the pilot was burnt to death. It was about four o'clock in the afternoon and we all rushed out of school to see it. One of my friends was terribly upset as the pilot had lodged at her house.

Bournemouth School for Boys at that time was in Portchester Road and the School for Girls at the Lansdowne. Later both schools moved out to Charminster. We girls from Bournemouth Girls used to meet the boys along Lansdowne Road on our way home from school and we would have little flirtations until we were spotted and reported to the headmistress by some old spoilsport. We girls used to wait for the Lansdowne clock to strike four o'clock and it was down pens and we'd all rush out of school, straight across the Lansdowne and Holdenhurst Roads to catch our trams without looking right or left. You can't imagine doing that today. I simply hated school and I've met another old girl in my village who has said exactly the same thing.

We had to buy all our own books in those days. We were reading *The Water Babies* for English. We were told to bring 2s 6d for *Alice Through the Looking Glass*. Well, my Dad, who had an awful job to pay for my school fees, wouldn't give me the money. He told me before I started at Bournemouth School, I couldn't expect to have the same as everyone else. He said I should finish reading *Water Babies* first. He was quite right, of course, but I was a snob and would not say my Dad could not afford it, so I kept saying I'd forgotten the money, this went on for some time. We got Order Marks for bad behaviour, so I got an Order Mark for forgetting. When you got four Order Marks you got a Conduct Mark and your name would go down in a black book which would "last 100 years". The 100 years is nearly up now. I'd love to have a peep in the black book and see if it still exists. My poor old Dad had to fork out in the end, but I had to sit in the Head's office for the rest of the term and read the blinking *Water Babies* and most of all miss my games which I loved and was very good at. I never really read the beastly book but just turned the pages over and although I have it in my book case, I have never read the thing.

We had to wear navy blue gym slips with velvet tops. Mine was made by an awful dressmaker from two skirts of my mother's. They were two different colour navies, one very dark and one purply navy and I used to go around with my arms clamped close to my sides so no one should see the two different blues, *and* I had to always stand by the daughter of a very good tailor in Winton who wore an immaculate gym slip. When we had new ones they always had to be measured to be two inches above the knee and our gym mistress used to come round with a tape measure and measure our gym slips and pin them up if they were not short enough.'

▣ ALDERHOLT SCHOOL ▣

'The school at Alderholt opened in 1874 and the first headmaster, Mr George Mann, with his very bushy beard, was here from 1874 to 1908.

All roads in the village were gravelled and to keep warm on the way to school younger children travelled in pairs – one was "horse" with knitted reins and his partner was the driver. Bigger girls had wooden hoops to "troll along", boys had iron ones. The boys wore hobnail boots and during the winter they would scuff a slide on the grass, pour water on it, then with a good frost at night it would be like an ice-rink in the morning!

There were no school dinners, of course, and the children took their own food. A cup of cocoa at the school cost twopence a week. Some of the older boys had to fill the kettles from the pump and heat the water on the open fires – they received twopence a week each for this.'

▣ STUDLAND VILLAGE SCHOOL ▣

'The headmistress at Studland was a First World War widow, married just six weeks before her young husband was killed on the Western Front.

Our village school was a lovely stone building of Victorian vintage, consisting of two rooms heated by an open fire in each room. Incorporated was the school house where the headmistress lived; this house faced south while the school looked west, east and north. One toilet for the girls and one for the boys, separated by a stone wall, all of seven foot! The number of pupils in varying ages was about 40 to

50, never higher. Religious education was excellent, with a hymn, prayers and reading to start every day. Scripture lessons were part of the curriculum, with testing and a yearly examination by the Rural Dean who lived at Langton. We had great fun making Biblical scenes with sand trays and plasticine.

The three Rs were rigorously adhered to in both junior and senior classrooms. Poetry and verse were explored, explained and learned. Music and singing (the lady organist from the church playing the piano for us) was taken for two periods each week. We had maths, history and geography, also spelling and mental arithmetic, from the word go! The fact that a different level of teaching to another group of children was going on at the same time as we were concentrating on our level and our learning appeared not to worry any of us. I cannot recall one incident of attention wandering to another group, even when reading!

We had a large playing field with a purpose-built level pitch for cricket, which we played with great enthusiasm. Our playground adjoined a farm field, where the cows gathered for afternoon milking. If a boundary was hit into the long field, the fielder had to vault over the stile and run in hot pursuit after the ball, a hazardous run between very soft and numerous cowpats which sometimes ended in disaster. I remember a fielder in hot pursuit egged on by his loud and cheering side, only to trip and fall face first among the cows' mud and cowpats. He was hauled back into the school field smothered, but grimly hanging onto the ball, what a hero! The boy did pong, and the

only remedy was to wash him down under the school pump. These games were organised by the older boys and girls, mostly boys, they made the rules, they were the umpires and the captains, but they didn't quite have the last word, the mistress had the whistle!

If going on to the new Swanage grammar school, one left the village school at age eleven. Living in a village the only means of transport was by cycle, the County gave a grant of £5 towards the cost of this. We would leave home at 8.30 am and arrive back at 4.30 pm. The cycle had a rack or carrier at the rear on which one strapped the school case containing homework books, pens, pencils etc, also packed lunch. Attaché cases, brown with two locks, could be obtained from Woolworths at the price of 6d. We all had one.

With about 30 pupils in a form, boys outnumbered girls, with usually about ten girls in the form. All males were called by their surnames. All teaching staff wore gowns at all times; they were always addressed as Sir or Miss. The headmaster and headmistress had a study each, and there were two staffrooms. We enjoyed large cloakrooms, toilets, washbasins, drinking fountains, large airy form rooms, and a desk and chair for our use during that school year, chosen to fit one's size and height! At the village school desks were long to accommodate four or six pupils, seating being on a fixed backless bench; a straight back was guaranteed.

We competed at school games, one house against the other, and we also competed against other schools and generally took enormous pride in our school. Founders Day was always observed. "Forty Years On" was our school song. Brown was the predominant colour in our school uniform. Yellow and red stockings were worn at all times, as also was the school hat; blouse sleeves were never to be rolled up.'

▨ A WALK ACROSS THE FIELDS ▨

'At Chedington in the late 1930s we had two teachers at one time, but later only one. I used to take the infants for reading and writing. The loos were only buckets. Children used to walk from the Beaminster Downs across the fields. We took sandwiches for dinner,

The serious business of conkers at Sticklands school, Evershot.

or walked home. School finished at 4 pm in the summer and 3.30 pm in the winter.'

◼ COOKERY CLASS ◼

'At Abbotsbury school in the 1930s we had a cookery class on Monday afternoon. It was held in an old chapel at the back of the school. The girls from Portesham school used to come over and join us. I can still see the great big kitchen range that we learned to cook on. On Wednesday afternoon the Portesham and Abbotsbury boys had a woodwork lesson in the same chapel.'

◼ CATTISTOCK CANE ◼

'Schooldays had a lasting effect on my memory. We had two very strict lady teachers and the head, Miss Seabrook, was a somewhat frightening person. I used to sit in a front double desk with a boy and because we had our desk lids up too long she slammed them down and gave us the cane. I don't know what she thought we were doing. During the war we had to practise wearing our gas masks, which became hot and uncomfortable. School days were very strict but we had a good grounding that stood us in good stead in later years.'

▣ AT LANGTON MATRAVERS ▣

'I went to the village school at Langton Matravers, just over the road. I loved school and stayed until I was nearly 15. Our headmaster was very strict, but very fair. There were two small playgrounds, one for the boys and one for the girls. I think one of our favourite games was marbles, there were several ways of playing this. We also did a lot of skipping and we had hoops, the girls' were made of wood and the boys' were made of iron. Our headmaster often used the cane, but I am sure this never did any harm, and the children were much better behaved in those days.

During the summer holidays we spent a lot of time in the hay fields, when the hay was turned several times before it was made in to hay ricks. We used to make houses in it and the farmers never minded us playing there as it probably helped to dry it out.'

▣ CANN SCHOOL IN THE 1940S ▣

'From 1941 to 1947 I was educated at Cann school, a Church of England primary school on the outskirts of Shaftesbury. A typical Victorian building, it had two classrooms, the infants' room and the "big room" divided by a sliding partition. There were two teachers, Miss Duden taught the infants and Mrs Edwards the juniors, around 60 pupils in all.

For a large part of my time there the school milk was delivered by the local farmer, poured from a churn into a large white enamelled pitcher and left in the kitchen. It was the task of the milk monitors during early morning lessons to pour this milk into cups which were

left on trays ready for morning break. The kitchen, which had once been part of the teacher's house, had a stone floor and a stone sink with a pump at the side and was often extremely damp. It was quite common on picking up the metal trays of cups, to find a slug nestling under the rim and once having drunk his milk a boy found a snail at the bottom of his cup! As I have always had a phobia about slugs and snails I dreaded this happening to me, but luckily it never did.

School dinners were cooked at the secondary modern school nearby and delivered to us in metal containers – trays for the meat, veg and sweet, and tall canisters for gravy and custard. The desks in the infants' room were put together to form tables and the oldest pupils waited on the younger ones. One of the teachers and a "dinner lady" served the food. One day the teacher was unwell and she asked me to serve in her place. I found the long handled spoon very difficult to manage and consequently was very slow. I was not very popular that day! I remember meals of minced meat, swede and potatoes, corned beef, mashed potato and beetroot but my most vivid memory is of chocolate sponge pudding made with soda, not bicarbonate of soda as you might expect but large pieces like washing soda. Every time you took a mouthful you crunched on these bitter tasting lumps, ugh!

I took my eleven-plus exam in 1947, the year of the big freeze. We had to go to the girls' high school to sit the exam. Mum came with me as I didn't know the way. I remember us walking the mile or so to Shaftesbury along the A30 on a sunny March morning with banks of melting snow on either side of the road and large pieces of ice falling from the electric cables overhead. I was still only ten when I took the

BRIDPORT GRAMMAR SCHOOL

SPEECH DAY

THURSDAY, NOVEMBER 13TH, 1941

AT 2.30 P.M.

Programme.

HYMN :   From Homes of Quiet Peace

Chairman's Remarks :   Alderman E. S. Reynolds, J.P.
(Chairman of the Governors)

Headmaster's Report.

SONG :   The Snowy Breasted Pearl   *Old Irish Melody*

Address :   A. J. Woodroffe, Esq., M.B.E., J.P.
(Vice-Chairman of the Dorset County Education Committee)

Distribution of Prizes.

SONG :   The Seas of England   *Charles Wood*
(Words by Walter de la Mare)

Vote of Thanks :   Proposed by J. O. Macdonald, Esq., J.P.
(Vice-Chairman of the Governors)

Seconded by Mrs. Howard
(Governor)

GOD SAVE THE KING

Speech day at Bridport Grammar School in 1941.

exam, which happily I managed to pass and I started at the high school on my eleventh birthday!

My name is Sylvia. While I was at primary school there was another girl called Sylvia at the school as well and by coincidence we shared the same birthday. As it was rather unusual to have two girls with the same name and the same birthday, each year our headmistress used to give us both a threepenny bit.'

▨ GETTING TO GRAMMAR SCHOOL ▨

'When I was eleven I passed my exam to go to the grammar school in Swanage. The village children travelled daily and what a long journey that seemed! The bus left Lulworth at 7.25 am and we collected children from other small villages on the way to Wareham. At the station we boarded the steam train for the ten mile journey to Swanage. The first formers were allocated a carriage and put in the care of their own "carriage leader", usually a sixth former or prefect. Being the "new boy/girl", you were often subjected to time honoured rituals, such as riding in the luggage rack, but it was all harmless fun and after a week or two you became "one of the crowd". Once at our destination, we had to board a bus to take us the mile and a half to the school. However, this was only a privilege for the girls. The boys had to walk whatever the weather.

At night, we had to repeat the journey in reverse, arriving home at 5.15. We then had an hour or two of homework to complete before the next day.

By 1960 it was decided that the Lulworth children should have a bus for the entire journey to Swanage, which made the day about 40 minutes shorter. I still journeyed on the steam train occasionally. When I played hockey for the school in 1964 to 1966 I had to make my own way to matches on a Saturday morning. I had to leave Lulworth on the 7.30 am bus, dressed in my brown school uniform, to catch the main line train from Wool station to Wareham. Then I transferred to the steam train to make my way to the school. I sometimes didn't get back home until 3 pm. All that for an hour's hockey match. I must have been keen!'

THE WORLD OF WORK

ON THE LAND

Farming was a way of life for many of us, and farm life in the first half of the century differed little from Victorian days. Horses still provided the power on the land and many farms were part of large estates, with the whole community involved in such busy times as haymaking and harvest.

▣ CHIEFLY AN AGRICULTURAL COUNTY ▣

'Dorset was chiefly an agricultural county and there was little industry except that associated with farming – waggon builders, blacksmiths and millers. In the early part of the century, practically all farms were part of large estates. The farms were let annually to farmers who often sublet dairies to other tenants whilst keeping sheep and arable farming as their own interest.

Dairies, usually of 50 or 60 cows, were rented to a man who often made Cheddar cheese or butter and Dorset blue cheese, a very hard dry cheese, and the whey or butter milk was used to fatten pigs. The farmer provided the cows with hay and cake during the year. The cows had to be in milk by 25th March, rented at about £10 each per annum.

The estate usually gave an annual rent dinner, often at the local inn, when all rents were paid and alterations in tenancies made. The farmers gave their workmen and wives a harvest supper and usually it was roast beef and Yorkshire pudding followed by apple pie and each man received a gold sovereign (no overtime was paid).

At the end of the war in 1918 large parts of estates were sold off and some large farms divided to provide smallholdings for men coming from the forces who wished to go into farming. The milking machine made a great difference in the dairy and also the cooler which reduced the temperature of the milk and helped in the keeping quality. United Dairies bought the milk at the farm, collected it and

126

used it for door to door delivery in towns or made it into cheese. Prices were very poor; one month in the summer of 1925 or 1926 the farmer was paid 4d for one gallon of milk.

Wages were about £1 10 shillings a week. The workmen's wives often helped in the fields by hoeing root crops, planting, picking up potatoes and stooking sheaves at harvest time.'

❈ THE FARM WORKER ❈

'My father worked at Manor Farm, Melbury Abbas as cowman, carter and general labourer. He was paid a sovereign for 14 days' work (including Saturdays and Sundays). Butter was 1s a pound, milk was 1d a pint and the rent 1s 6d a week.

There were no unions for agricultural workers until just before the Second World War. If you wanted a pay rise, you went to the Boss individually and asked for one. He might give you an extra 6d a week and he might not. There was no unemployment in those days. The farmers were employing so many more men then. On most of the

The staff of Bovington Farm in 1912.

127

farms there were eight to ten men employed. Machinery has killed the labour on the farms. The horses did a better job on the land than today's machinery does.

I left school at 14 in 1913 and went to work on the farm and worked from 6 am to 6 pm at 5s a week and I had to work on Sundays. I had to work alongside the men, keeping up with them and do the garden. I did the separating of the milk and made the butter, washed out the milk separator and put it all back together for the next use, morning and night. I also helped do the milking, and fed the pigs and calves. The cows stayed inside in the winter. Sometimes the cows were kept in the field at the top of Zigzag Hill and were rounded up to be milked up there, but of course farmers didn't keep as many cows then, about 20 was the usual number. The sheep were grazed up on the hills over a wide area and there was always a shepherd up there with them, sleeping in a hut. He used to grow turnips and kale and so on, for the sheep to eat, and they were hurdled into folds.

I left Manor Farm getting 35s a week, and went to another farm as a carter on 52s. But I had to walk the horses all day. Then when the farmer moved to another village I decided not to go with him. I left farm work and worked for a builder as a mason's labourer. I carried mortar to eight masons and I had to run much of the time. When it was up the scaffolding I had to carry it on my shoulder. We worked twelve hours a day and I was paid 1s an hour. It was a hard life. After three years I went back to working for a farmer and did timber hauling. He also had a mill and we collected sacks of wheat and barley from Semley station. Then in 1936, the farmer sold the farm.

Within a week I was working for the County Council where I worked for 27 years doing tarmacking. Sometimes, 50 or 60 tons of tarmac a day was delivered and this had to be all spread by hand, by two spreaders at a time. We had to go to work in Blandford, eleven miles, by push bike. Then one day the County surveyor came with the District surveyor to see us. He asked us how we got to work. When we told him, he said that if we did that we wouldn't be fit for a day's work and that in future we should have a lorry to bring us to work.'

◼ 'THE LITTLE DAIRIES' ◼

'I was born in 1916 in the heart of the Blackmore Vale and grew up on a farm rather like those described by Thomas Hardy in his novels as "the little dairies". Here we kept cattle, pigs, poultry and horses, the latter of course being quite a work force before the days of tractors. My grandfather also did a bit of horse breeding and supplied some for the army in the Great War.

In the dairy were large pans of milk which stood overnight to be skimmed in the morning with a brass skimmer. The cream was retained in a large stone crock for buttermaking and the skimmed milk was fed to the calves or pigs. Grandfather made butter for the house using a hand-turned wooden churn. The bulk of the milk was taken to a local factory for cheesemaking. In later years, however, it was collected by lorry and taken to the Cow and Gate factory at Sherborne.

Horses played a big part in the work. Hay was cut by horse-drawn mowing machines, corn was cut by a binder requiring three horses to pull it. A horse pulled the various implements used in haymaking: side rake, swath turner, tedder, horse rake and waggons. A horse pulled the plough, roller, cultivator, chain harrow and the muck-spreading putt. For social visiting my grandfather drove a four wheel phaeton but a spring van sufficed for visiting the market town of Sturminster Newton.

This, then, was life on a mixed farm in the Blackmore Vale until the mid 1920s. Then my father bought his first tractor, a secondhand Fordson, the beginning of mechanisation for Manor Farm. He retired in the early 1930s and soon after that came mains water, electricity and general modernisation.'

◼ TELEGRAMS AND AERIALS ◼

'In the 1920s a local farmer had an arrangement with the Meteorological Office during the haymaking season, so that whenever a change in the weather was expected they would send him a telegram to inform him what to expect. He would place it on the gate next to the road.

Other farmers came to read it to see if it was safe to mow the grass, and whether the dry weather would continue.

He owned a wood of young ash saplings, and made quite a lot of money selling these as poles to hold up the wireless aerials, a new invention just coming in.'

▣ TURNING THE HAY ▣

'In the summer on our farm at Chedington, Father used the horses for mowing and we children had to use hand rakes to turn the grass and when it was dry help to make hay ricks. We also helped Mother take the tea into the fields.'

▣ LAMBING AND ALL ▣

'I left school at twelve in 1916 and worked for Mr Diffey at West Down Farm, Lulworth, looking after 200 ewes, doing lambing and all. I got five shillings for working seven days a week. My father got eleven shillings. The rent on our house was one shilling a week.'

▣ ABOUT 57 ACRES ▣

'I came to Leigh in 1923 and lived in the cottage opposite the bakery. The farm was about 57 acres, we milked about 30 cows in the summer and 25 in the winter. The cows were mostly shorthorns and were milked by hand, the milk put into churns and taken to Yetminster milk factory by horse and waggon. It was then put into tanks and taken by train to London. Once a week after unloading the milk my father went to a railway siding and loaded the waggon with animal feed, which was in hessian sacks. He also bought slabs of linseed cake; this was put into a cake cracker to feed the cows and horses.

There weren't any milk coolers or fridges and in the summer I remember my father damming the stream and standing the churns of evening milk in the water for the night. There wasn't any running water on the farm, most of the fields had ponds in them, and in the

An early tractor in action at Melbury Abbas.

winter the ice had to be broken twice a day for the cows to be able to drink. Most of these dried up in the summer and we had to take churns to the ford at Chetnole and fill them with a bucket. Two people usually did this, one standing in the water, filling the bucket and handing it up to someone in the waggon, who poured it into the churns. It was then brought back to the farm and poured into the cattle troughs.

We had three horses, two were big cart horses which my grandfather had bought in 1919 from the War Office, they had been used for pulling big guns in France in the 1914/18 war. They both had a broad arrow branded on their shoulders; one was called Captain, the other Colonel. The other horse was a small Welsh black cob called Bob, he was used to pull the milk cart and two-wheeled trap.

Calves that were not wanted for the dairy were taken by horse and waggon to the Sherborne market, which took place where the old market car park is now. The calves were put into pens and sold by Senior & Godwin, the auctioneers. The horse and cart was then driven to Pigby Road, to the old Pigby Hotel, where there were a lot of stables, and handed to the ostler, who was given 6d. His job was to feed the horse from the nosebag, which my father had brought, and give it a bucket of water; he was told by my father what time to get it harnessed for the return journey. If my father had bought any pigs at the market he had to drive the cart back up the market, load them and bring them home.

We always had a lot of laying hens (all free range). We bought day old chicks from a Mr Hannan at Holmbushes Farm, about 100 at a time, and always bought 25 day old cockerels which were fattened and eaten by us. Those day-olds were put in a "foster mother", a box-like contraption with a paraffin lamp in it to keep them warm. The eggs were taken in boxes to the Carpenter's Arms where a carrier, Mr Smith and later Mr Charles, took them to Dorchester market. They were sold by auction to bakers and hoteliers.

I had to help with some of the farm jobs, feeding chickens and helping to clean the horses out once a week. The job I really enjoyed was when one of the horses had to have new shoes. The blacksmith was Mr Bridle. My father used to put me on the horse (bare backed) and I took it to the smithy, where a piece of iron was heated and shaped into a horse shoe, by knocking it with a big hammer on the anvil. The fire to heat the iron was kept alight by a pair of big bellows. I then rode the horse home.

Haymaking time was a very busy one, all working from daylight till dark. My father used to start mowing the grass at 4.30 am as the sun hadn't risen and the flies weren't about to tease the horses. The day was mainly spent shaking and drying the grass, then after the evening's milking it was all hands on deck. My job was to see the jars of cider were kept full. The hay was loaded by hand into a waggon, then taken to the rickyard to be put into ricks.

This work was done not only by the farmer and the farm labourers, but by all able-bodied people that had other trades by day. They were called strappers. Some worked on the railway at Yetminster, you didn't ask them to come they just turned up for the extra money. They were paid 6d per hour and as much cider as they could drink plus a supper of bread and cheese. Their wages were kept by the farmer until the men collected the money and most of them walked to Sherborne to the fair, where they bought winter clothes for themselves and their families and spent the rest on beer at the numerous pubs in town. The farm labourers were always given the next day off work, not I might add out of kindness from the farmer, but because most of them were legless by the time they had spent their money and would not have been able to do much work if they got home, but by the time they'd got back to Leigh (about midnight) they were cold sober and would turn up for work the next day.

We were almost self supporting, having our own milk and eggs, and my mother made our butter. We had sows and their litters were fattened and sold to a bacon factory near Yeovil. We had a pig killed in October at the bacon factory. We kept half, which they cured so we always had bacon. When the house pig was killed, Mrs Dewland took the offal and made faggots, black pudding and "chiddlings" from it. My father farmed at Brookside Farm until he retired in 1967.'

▣ HARVEST BUGS ▣

'As a child in the 1930s I spent my summer holidays in Milton Abbas with my grandmother, but for one week I went to stay with my cousins during the harvesting. We would take cold tea up for the men in the afternoon and ride home on the backs of the horses. On returning to my grandmother's I was always very itchy and Gran used to say, "Come on, my girl, a vinegar bath for you to get rid of the harvest bugs." It always did the trick.'

▣ THE DAIRY AT WOOLCOMBE FARM ▣

'In 1940 my grandfather and father rented the dairy at Woolcombe Farm, near Toller Porcorum. I had to help hand milk at weekends and school holidays, which I enjoyed. We used the three-legged stool and open bucket, and in winter it was a joy to snuggle up to the warm flanks of a cow and hear the "ping, ping" of the milk into the empty bucket, gradually changing as more milk poured into the pail. The smell of good hay with the cows happily munching from the mangers evokes many memories. The milk was tipped into the ten gallon churn (which had replaced the old 17 gallon one then) through a strainer containing a gauze pad, no sterilisation, hand washing or udder washing! In summer the churns were put in a tank of water supplied from a spring to keep cool. I never remember any being returned as poor from the factory. After milking the churns had to be loaded into the waggon and taken by horse to the road for the collection by the boy from the milk stand.

In those days the cows were only fed hay to supplement grass during the winter so most calved in the spring in time for the new grass. Haymaking was done by horse-driven machinery, and I remember having to keep the horse walking round and round the pole to drive the elevator to put the hay on the side, which later had to be thatched.'

▨ IN THE CIDER ▨

'I grew up on the edge of the Blackmore Vale. On the way home from school in the late summer we were able to watch the old men making cider in a press made from an old mangle. This was a cider area where much was made on the farms. It was said that when the apples were shovelled up, no account was taken of a few cow pats or rotten fruit. It all went into the mill and when the cider was maturing in large barrels, it was customary to feed it. Rotten meat was a favourite. At one farm the barrels were open topped, left underneath the hen roost. If one fell in no one was the wiser until the barrels were cleaned, then maybe there would emerge a few talons and beaks.'

▨ PIGS AND MINK ▨

'I moved to Child Okeford with my husband and young son on 6th June 1946. My husband had been asked to start a herd of pedigree saddleback pigs at Okeford Fitzpaine. The dairies there used to belong to Edward Philips & Son and were just taken over by Malmsbury & Parsons Davies of Bournemouth. One of the Parsons brothers was very interested in pedigree pigs and through the National Pig Breeders Association my husband was asked to help.

My husband did manage to establish a prize-winning herd of pigs. He named them the "Phipson Herd" after the man who owned the cheesemaking milk factory before. He took his sows and boars to all the big agricultural shows and won a lot of prizes, including championships.

Mink coats became a dream for every woman after the Queen and Princess Margaret were given one by the Canadian mink farmers. This started my husband off on mink farming. I had an uncle in Canada and he put us in touch with a mink farmer who came from Bournemouth. So we started a mink farm in the back garden, called Windmill Mink Farm. As it grew and we prospered we bought five and a half acres of woodland in Child Okeford. The reason for the name Windmill was that at Child Okeford at the foot of Hambledon Hill there was a windmill that used to take water up to the manor house. Just after we moved in, in about 1957 the windmill was removed and a pump house installed. The Windmill Mink Farm produced many pelts for export, which at the time the country badly needed. We employed local people, at one time six, so it helped the local people, but eventually, owing to bad publicity for the fur trade, the mink farm closed.'

◼ Milk to the Factory ◼

'My father was manager of the milk factory in East Road, Bridport. Local farmers brought their milk into the factory in churns, very often in a putt drawn by a horse. Others, further away like Chideock and the Marshwood Vale, had their milk collected from their farms by one of three lorries, each of which did two rounds a day. Some of the milk was pasteurised and sent by tanker to large towns and cities, the rest was separated and the cream was tinned, packed and despatched for marketing. Quite a large staff was employed.'

Before and after the milking machine – just one of the ways mechanisation cut the numbers to find work on the farms.

'Time on a farm was never idle, even children had daily tasks allocated to them. While still at Cattistock school we were sent home from twelve to two o'clock, giving the teachers time to cook and eat their lunch. Sometimes before school but always afterwards I had to help hand-milk the 40 cows.

Water was not piped across the fields at that time and animals were brought off the hills every day to drink from the pond or stream. The milk was collected by the Maiden Newton dairy in ten gallon churns and sent off by train to London in big tankers. Before and after the war the dairy also made cheese. We put back some of the milk to turn the cream into butter with the help of a big wooden churn, the remainder was fed to pigs and calves. There is no dairy farmer in Chilfrome today, but at that time cows were milked at the following farms: Lancombe, Heaven, Grovestall, Home Farm (my home before marriage), Sticklands and Chilfrome House and Chilfrome Cottage. Cattle were sold at our local market in Dorchester, and Bridport also held a weekly cattle market.

Most of the work on the farm was done with horses, but eventually we were the proud owners of a Standard Ford tractor, no tyres but steel wheels with spade lugs.

As food was in short supply every farm had to plough up a certain acreage for wheat and potatoes. Ministry inspectors had the power to turn farmers off their land if the farm was not managed properly. We also grew mangolds and kale for the cattle, the former being overwintered in clamps.

Haymaking involved many people, the hay being fed into the elevator to form a rick which needed thatching for winter protection. This hay was later cut out by hand and carted off by horse and waggon. Corn was cut by binder and put into ricks, also thatched. Threshing was a major operation, a steam powered threshing machine was hired for the occasion. The wheat straw was tied into bundles for use as thatch, barley and oat straw put back into a rick and thatched for later use as bedding and feed.

Hedges were laid which provided wood for the fire. To keep the rabbit population under control we caught them by netting, wires and with ferrets. Sheep dipping was compulsory, the local policeman came to watch, and Chilfrome sheep wash was used before shearing.'

▨ A DORSET FARMHOUSE IN THE 1950S ▨

'For a 16 year old girl in a Dorset farmhouse in the mid 1950s Monday washday meant a seven o'clock start. After lunch we had to go and make up beds, dust and mop bedrooms and then start getting the washing in from the line. It all had to be folded neatly and square-cornered things squared up. This done it was put in a basket and left until Tuesday.

Tuesday was not quite so hectic but still pretty busy. We always made our own butter so first thing after breakfast every day the milk which had been standing for a day in the cold dairy had to be heated over a pan of water to separate the cream from the buttermilk. Then it was upstairs to clean the bedrooms, which was quite different than it is today, mostly rugs and lino on the floors. Rugs had to be shaken, bedrooms brushed, polished and then mopped before putting all back tidy. Bathrooms always had to have a good wipe down. By this time, it was time to get the lunch ready. After lunch the ironing had to be done and put away.

Wednesdays and Sundays were always the buttermaking days. We used to make the butter by stirring the cream with our bare hands that we had scrubbed and chilled. It didn't take long to turn to butter as it was thick clotted cream. After it turned to butter the buttermilk was topped off and then it was rinsed in cold water until the water ran clear. When this happened we would put salt in and then rinse again, then we would get all the water out and pat up in half pound packs of butter.

We always had a lot of cakes and scones in the house that were all home-made. We did not buy bread except at Easter when we made saffron bread, cakes and Chelsea buns. The rest of the week was equally busy, one big task everyday, cleaning and polishing other rooms and brass cleaning. We also did the flower gardens when the weather was fine, in bad weather we always had painting to do, or we would wash and pack the eggs ready for the packing station and put some in buckets of waterglass for use in the winter when the hens stopped laying.

Christmas time we always had a lot of poultry to get ready for customers. We couldn't do this too early as there were no deep freezers then. This often used to be finished Christmas Eve. During the year we would have a pig killed, this had to be salted and packed in earthenware jars to keep it. The offal and head had to be cooked up to make faggots and brawn, the pig's trotters were scrubbed and boiled. Of course, we had rabbit but that was always fresh, as my father used to go and catch one when anyone wanted one. I always went with him, either to carry the light if it was in the dark, or stand over the hole by the net to catch the rabbit when it bolted out of the burrow in the daylight.

I had to work seven days a week with one Sunday off once a month to go to church. I had to cycle about four miles each way every day, whatever the weather, for £2 10s a week. Life was very satisfying then and just as good as it is today.'

VILLAGE TRADES AND CRAFTS

Most people worked close to their homes, and villages were busy with day to day life. Much employment was tied to the land, perhaps through crafts such as those of the blacksmith and wheelwright, but there were many other ways we made a living locally.

▨ QUIET CORFE CASTLE ▨

'My family went to live in Corfe Castle in 1922 when I was ten years old, so I remember the village when it was a quiet, self supporting place with very little traffic. There were only three cars in the village, one owned by the doctor and the others were taxis. If we wanted to go further afield we either walked, bicycled when we got older, or went by train or taxi. The railway was our great lifeline, bringing in supplies of all sorts, whatever goods were needed, including coal and groceries; it also transported cattle to market, and there was a very busy milk factory adjacent, to which the local farmers brought their milk daily, where it was processed and sent off to London by rail.

One could get all one required for daily living in the village. There were five grocer's shops, two bakers, one butcher, one draper's where you could get a wide miscellany of things, a little shop which sold boots and shoes, and one where you could get them repaired; two coal men, a sweep and an oil man – most important as all lighting was by oil lamp, and some heating and cooking by oil too; he also sold soap and brushes and other hardware, and toured the Purbeck villages with horse and cart, later by van. The bakers also delivered by horse and cart, in the village and beyond, and I remember running down to meet the baker's cart on Good Friday morning to get hot cross buns for our breakfast which had been baked overnight. One of the bakers baked the bread in the old faggot ovens, burning the faggots in the oven, then clearing the ashes and putting the bread dough in to cook in the heat.

There were two building firms who employed quite a number of men – carpenters, masons, bricklayers and labourers when building was starting after the 1914–18 war. The builders were also undertakers, so with a resident doctor and two monthly nurses the population was looked after from the cradle to the grave. There were three local farmers who delivered milk once or twice a day, still warm from the cow, unpasteurised, and there was quite a lot of tuberculosis about locally. There was even a little shop where you could get men's clothing, about the only things one had to leave the village for were household furnishings and outdoor clothes.

Besides all the employment locally in the shops and businesses, a lot of men worked in the local clay mines, and some went daily to

Holton Heath cordite factory by train. Farming also employed a lot of men in the area, as tractors were unknown, and work on the land was done using horses. That reminds me, there were two blacksmiths and a saddler in the village at that time. Time has certainly made many changes to village life in the last 70 years.'

◪ ALDERHOLT FAMILIES ◪

'Alderholt is situated only two miles from Fordingbridge and belonged to the lord of the manor of Cranborne – the family have always taken a very keen interest in the village.

Local industries at Alderholt, apart from farming, included brick-making at Sandleheath brickyard. The grandfather of a present resident walked two miles to work and stayed there all night. In the evening his two grandchildren, aged six and nine years, walked to the

Taking away shingle at West Bay.

brickyard to take his supper – boiled bacon, cabbage and potato, followed by boiled apple dumpling, all in a basin in a rush basket. The children were allowed to climb the ladder at the end of the kitchen and look at the haze from the fire. When the fire cooled, they were allowed to walk along the brick walk at the top of the kiln. Brickmaking also went on at the top of Park Lane. All broken brick was used to make up Park Lane itself and the brick was still there until the road was tarmacked in the 1970s.

There were potteries down near the Salisbury Arms, now a farm. Inkwells were made for the Stevens Ink Company, and clay pipes and broken pottery have been found in the area.

The Lane family made hurdles and spars, which were sold in the area. There were off-licences at the Salisbury Arms and the Red Lion. At the Cranborne end of the village is Goldoak Farm which still has marked on its wall "Gold Oak Bar". The brewers were Hopgood & Sons, Wimborne Ales.

General Archibald Wavell, father of the Viceroy of India, lived in the village and employed local girls in the house. He died at the age of 92 in 1936 and all members of his household who had spent two years or more in his employ were left £2 for each year. One local girl received £8 with which she bought a new bicycle – Royal Enfield Sports model!

Early on there was always a resident policeman. At one time he ran a youth club in the reading room – he whacked anyone who misbehaved with a billiard cue. Periodically he would disappear off round the village on his bicycle to round up any wrongdoers, then came back to the youth club.

There were many thriving businesses in the past, sadly reduced because of the growth of supermarkets. From the grocer's and baker's at Pressies Corner hot cross buns were delivered all round the village at 5 am on Good Friday. Orders were collected for groceries on Monday and the goods delivered next day by horse and cart. There were three butchers, all of whom delivered meat. Fish was brought from Poole and the man walked round the village pushing his truck and shouting "Fish for sale!" There was a haberdashery shop and newsagent, a shoe mending shop and a small garage next to the post office.'

▨ Cattistock in 1915 ▨

'The Cattistock of 80 years ago was much more self sufficient than today.

The inner man was well catered for with two grocery shops – the high-class Paul's Grocery Stores below Millers Barton and Roger's General Stores and Bakery on the site of the present shop, where you could buy almost anything including kaolin for a poultice to treat pneumonia or boils.

Bread was an important part of the diet supporting two other bakeries – one in Orchard Cottage and the family business of Fudges in Bun House (still in existence at Leigh).

The east end of Bell House housed a butcher's shop which soon became a fish shop. Milk was supplied by the farms and the Dewdney family of Sandhills Farm delivered from two buckets carried on a yoke – no pasteurisation then! Or you could collect your milk, along with a jar of cider, from Mrs Dawe's dairy at the Fox and Hounds Inn.

Hooper's of Manor Farm sent milk to the United Dairy factory on milk carts, although the farm was mainly arable with sheep on the hills. Mr Spicer farmed in the centre of the village to the east of the Fox and Hounds and Cattistock Mill, run by the Beater family, provided meal for the livestock and maize and corn for the villagers' poultry.

The hardware and gift shop run by Mr Tizzard was at the east end of Duck Street. Everyone could be well turned-out by Mr Williams, the tailor in the square, Mr Aves the cobbler behind Bun House and Mrs Nobbs the dressmaker sitting in her bay window at Corner Cottage, whilst Mrs Pugsley took in laundry.

The post office was opposite Mill Close and you could hire a waggonette to take you to the station from Mrs Birch at Millers Barton – described by the children as an old witch.

Horses were the only means of transport so there were two

blacksmith/farriers, one in Mill Lane (which survived until 1968) run by Mr Bowles and later by the Hatchers. The other one was next to the stables and two horses are still to be seen painted on the wall. This soon became a garage run by Bert Harwood who was a modern young man and generated electricity which he supplied to the Fox and Hounds and Pound House in the 1930s.

Bert's father was the village undertaker, wheelwright, carpenter and decorator running his business from Cattistock House. Abel Harvey next door was a builder and decorator with the slogan "Abel by name – able by nature". The kennels were well established and the kennelman's name was Riggs.

There was a midwife (Mrs Hatcher) to deliver the babies, the Rev Stickland to baptise them, Mrs Brown the schoolmistress to educate them and a village bobby to ensure their safety.

There was employment on the farms, in the businesses and in the house and gardens of Cattistock Lodge under the head gardener George Brind.

There was entertainment in the old barn at Prospect Farm and convivial company after a hard day's work in the Fox and Hounds. Life in Cattistock provided everything the inhabitants required.'

▦ A SMALL MARKET TOWN ▦

'Gillingham was a busy small market town in 1938 with brickworks, BP, Shell and Esso depots and a milk factory in New Road.

In Station Road we had the railway, Oake Woods bacon factory, the glue factory, a large milk factory, the Hudson & Martin timber yard, the glove factory, two garages, shops, printing works and every week a cattle market was held in the yard of the Market Hall; the Market Hall was used for dances and functions.

The High Street had a lot of shops and houses and the town mill; the shops in the square included International Stores, Slades Outfitters and Samways the chemist. There were shops in Queen Street including the Co-op. We had six butcher's shops and six grocery shops and six gents' and ladies' outfitters. We had three tennis courts to play on, a recreation ground and a grammar school. There was one swimming pool, which belonged to the grammar school. On the Ham Road, Hines had a lorry depot.

There were several farms around the town but a lot of the fields are built on now. The new school in Hardings Lane was opened in 1941. The gas works was in Gas Lane, the gas showroom and office in the High Street.'

▣ Gloving ▣

'My mother joined other village women who knitted gloves as a home industry. They mostly used a yarn called silkette, which was very hardwearing, and there were two patterns, one of which was called Ringwood. Sometimes they used yellow wool, which I understood was for linings. They made these gloves for a firm in Yeovil and an agent from Blandford came to collect and pay and to supply further materials. At that time (the 1940s) the payment was one shilling a pair. My mother used to press me to knit some cuffs, which I wasn't very keen on but had to do. Some women took their knitting everywhere, they could even walk along the village street happily knitting away. They never seemed to look at what they were doing, and I should think they could even manage it in their sleep!'

▣ Stone Quarries ▣

'All the lanes at Acton, near Langton Matravers, were of crushed stones and the lime quarry, the stone quarries and farming seemed to be the main industries. My grandfather had his own quarry and my uncle and cousins worked there until the outbreak of war in 1939. It is an industry that has been continued by many others, and Harris, Brown and Landen are very old names too.'

▣ Church Knowle Post Office ▣

'The first post office in Church Knowle was started by Mrs Emily Manuel in the late 1800s. She was widowed twice with young children to bring up. Colonel Mansell the landowner, of whose estate

'Grandfather Harris and Uncle Sam' in the stone quarry near Langton Matravers.

Church Knowle was then still a part, suggested she start the post office for a wage of half-a-crown a week. A fire which started in an adjoining cottage destroyed her cottage too. She moved into her father's cottage and, in a small room next to the cowshed, continued the post office, supplementing her wages by making home-made sweets.

After serving as postmistress for over 40 years she handed over to her daughter Joy who continued in the post for almost another 40 years. She in turn was succeeded by her daughter-in-law Mary who has carried on the family tradition in the same way for the past 25 years, retiring only very recently.'

OTHER WAYS WE MADE A LIVING

On the coast and inland, there were dozens of other ways we made our living. These are just a few examples, from running a daily delivery round, to paddle steamers, to nursing in the workhouse.

☒ THE TELEPHONE EXCHANGE AT CHARMOUTH ☒

'At the corner of Barr Lane, facing Lower Sea Lane, is Charmouth Lodge with a small pink cottage nestled close by its side. At the lodge lived the three Whittington sisters with their brother, all descendants of Dick Whittington! The brother was a canon. Until after the last war, the sisters ran a small private school called The Limes in the pink thatched cottage.

Further up the Street, on the south side just beyond the library, is Langley House, a double-fronted property which was once the ironmonger's, run by Miss Child. Prior to that, just before and during the war, the shop was a sub-post office and a stationer's run by Mr and Mrs Holly which also housed the two-mornings-a-week Lloyds bank and the Charmouth telephone exchange! The exchange was a tiny switchboard at the back of the shop, with just a few lines . . . the doctor's telephone number was 3, Dampiers' was 4, Mrs Pass out at Wootton was 2. The two shop assistants served in the shop and helped on the switchboard. The telephone exchange also took the fire calls! There were no fire alarms in the village, although later on a break-the-glass alarm was installed outside the fire station.'

☒ TELEPHONES IN DORCHESTER ☒

'I was a part-time telephonist at Dorchester, who commenced service in 1935 and retired as a chief supervisor in 1977.

In London one of the earliest exchanges was in Chancery Lane in 1879, with about 100 subscribers. In Bournemouth the first line was

147

established in 1884, and by 1886 a group of about 30 businesses and professional people were connected. In Dorchester it is said to have started with a switchboard at the King's Arms Hotel in High East Street. In 1899 a switchboard was installed at 4 Cedar Park Villas, a red brick terraced house in Trinity Street later demolished to make way for Marks and Spencer.

This small exchange came about by an agreement between the National Telephone Company and a Mrs Churchouse. In the agreement it was stipulated "that an allowance of two shillings a week be paid to reasonably and sufficiently light and heat the premises, using gas only as an illuminant". At that time there were eleven subscribers, and the number had only risen to 170 by 1926 when the exchange was transferred to the head post office in a room overlooking South Street.

This must have been a temporary measure while a new three storey building was erected on the corner of Trinity Street and New Street. On the top floor was the new telephone exchange which was opened on 1st April 1926 with 240 subscribers. It had seven positions; part was for incoming calls from other exchanges, and on the other positions was subscribers' own labelled calling equipment. This was a central battery exchange, which meant that batteries were no longer required at subscribers' premises.

Unlike today when you phone the sales department to arrange the installation of a telephone, then a sales representative was employed to visit likely customers to persuade them it would be an advantage to have a phone installed.

In those days calls up to, I believe, 15 miles were not timed, and some calls lasted a very long time. These calls were charged according to the distance away from the exchange. Coloured rings of green, orange and red reminded operators how many times to press the meter key. Tickets were prepared for timed calls.

During this time in villages, switchboards were installed in sub post offices. Even today the deep friendly voice of Mr P at one office is still remembered by ex-telephonists, and the irritable tone of Mrs B at another, as if she had been interrupted while mixing up a cake!

Some village operators gave unusual advice to callers: "No, you won't get Mrs So and So, she has just gone up the street." This personal touch disappeared when small automatic exchanges were built in the villages.

In 1930 the service at Dorchester was slow to develop, and only three full-time operators were employed during the day time, working a 48 hour week. In 1935 the work justified an increase in staff, but only a part-time operator was required.

Over the years the exchange grew to 19 positions, filling the switch room; then there were 2,500 subscribers. It closed on the 30th May 1969, when the new automatic exchange opened in South Walks Road.'

▣ THE ESTATE OFFICE AT EAST LULWORTH ▣

'The war brought me to Lulworth. It was July 1941, and I came to say goodbye to my new young husband before he went overseas with his regiment, the Dorset Light Infantry. He was killed in action in January 1942. I was planning then to go back to Newcastle on Tyne, my home town, when a chance meeting with Mr Ian Macdonald, agent to the Weld Estate, resulted in the offer of a secretarial job in the estate office in East Lulworth, in the park near the castle which had burnt down in 1929.

This was a complete change for me, having spent my working life in a busy railway station, Newcastle on Tyne. One of my tasks was to collect some rents in East Lulworth and Coombe Keynes. This was a monthly chore; most tenants came to the estate office each month to pay their rent. The collections were made by bicycle, as I had never learned to drive, and anyway there wasn't much petrol around.

There were frequent cups of tea consumed as I called at the cottages, which made the job last longer than my boss expected! I was often taken aback at the primitive conditions of some of the cottages, now thankfully brought up to modern standards.

For a time I lived with Mrs Drew in the Old Rectory in Coombe Keynes, and the walk across the park to the office each morning and evening was sheer joy. When I eventually moved into my house in the park, adjoining the castle and the office, it was a great pleasure to see peacocks strutting around, sometimes displaying their beautiful plumage. These peacocks were the remaining survivors of those which lived around the castle, but sadly numbers diminished after it was burnt down.'

◼ A DAILY DELIVERY ROUND ◼

'My father, Percy Green, was born the youngest of 14 children in a small thatched cottage at Stoborough. He attended the village school and, on leaving, worked in a Wareham shop, finally as a delivery man.

In his late twenties he decided he would prefer to be his own boss. He borrowed £50 from his father, bought a van, equipped it with sundry hardware items and paraffin and proceeded to build up a daily

Percy Green's delivery van covered a wide area in the 1920s.

delivery round. This covered a large area, from Lulworth, Wool, Coombe Keynes on Monday, Lytchett Minster and Matravers and as far as Upton, Church Knowle, Furzebrook, Arne and even Wareham on a Saturday. It was a very busy life leaving at eight o'clock in the morning and returning around five thirty. Every evening the lorry, which by this time had replaced the original van, had to be restocked ready for the next day.

I well remember having to weigh pounds of soapflakes into brown paper bags from large paper sacks. Another task was unpacking china from wooden crates. To me, as a young child, it was like a lucky dip plunging my arms into the protective straw to see what treasure next appeared.

Some of our customers lived in quite isolated places. I still recall one lady who wore long black skirts, smoked a clay pipe, and spoke the broadest Dorset dialect that we could not always understand.

In more recent times when I have reminisced with people who were children at that time, they said that the day that the paraffin man called was one of the highlights of their week. He was always jolly and loved to have a joke with them.

In severe winter weather he was concerned that elderly customers who needed paraffin to light their homes or cook with were not supplied. On these occasions our little car was pressed into service if the roads were too snowed up to risk taking the lorry out.

When war came Dad was called up to serve in the army. Mum,

with the help of someone to drive the lorry, continued to run the business. During this time there were the added problems of having to deal with soap coupons and having great difficulty in obtaining saucepans or buckets to sell.

Dad returned from the war and took up the reins again but in a comparatively short time we were to see the beginnings of supermarket shopping and with many people becoming more mobile, there was no longer the same demand. The gradual decline in this kind of trading saw the beginning of the end of a particular way of life, not only for us, but all the people we had served over the years.'

▣ DORSET POLICE LIFE ▣

'I was born into a large police family in 1921. My grandfather had just retired after 30 years' service in the Dorset Constabulary and my father and four of his brothers joined this force after serving in the regular Army before and during the First World War.

Discipline was strict, single men lived in single quarters, looked after by a police matron, the wife of a fellow officer, and permission had to be obtained from a higher ranking officer if they wished to leave their quarters when off duty. Married men had to live in police houses or stations and notify their superiors when they were out of their district when off-duty.

After receiving their pay (in cash), the men, at Poole at least, were drilled by my father (an ex-Sergeant Major) in the large yard behind Market Street police station. This kept the men smart; the minimum height was 5 feet 10 inches and many of them topped this. They were seen on the beat at all times, working a 48 hour week, with a rest day, progressing through the days of the week until the seventh week brought a much welcomed weekend.

Overtime was not paid, but time off given in lieu, in the earlier days. Town beats were mostly walked and country beats cycled. However, my grandfather walked his, being expected to walk twelve miles to Dorchester, do market duty all day and then walk twelve miles back to his station and any problems awaiting him there.

Before the Second World War police wives were not allowed to work or own a business. Before they could marry a policeman they were "character assessed" to see if they were suitable to be police wives. In the country districts they often answered the phone and dealt with members of the public when their husbands were out; myself included, as I married a policeman. In the 1920s and 1930s men had to wait five years, later reduced to three, before marrying.

After the Second World War all this changed, of course, gradually policemen were allowed to live in their own houses and pay and conditions improved enormously.

However, the policemen of my young days were proud of their calling and devotion to duty and were loved and respected by the public.'

◼ Apprenticed to a Book Shop ◼

'When I started work in the 1920s I was apprenticed in a book shop for three years. The first year I was paid 1s 6d a week, the second year 2s 6d, the third year 3s 6d, and then my wages went up to £1 a week. I was there for ten years and then went to a chemist's where I earned £1 7s 6d a week. I felt I was in clover.'

◼ In a Solicitor's Office ◼

'When I left school in the 1920s at Bournemouth, I worked in a solicitor's office, earning 15 shillings a week. I had to pay Mum ten shillings and had five shillings for myself and had to dress myself on that and even save a bit. We often used to have to work until eight o'clock at night as we had to wait for the boss to come back from the courts and sign his letters. Then we put them through a copy book, addressed the envelopes and stamped them to take round to the post office.'

◼ Post Twice Daily ◼

'As a newcomer to Holwell in 1955 I was most impressed to find we had two deliveries of Her Majesty's mail every day. These were made by Violet, who lived in Bishops Caundle and tramped her round of 13 miles twice daily.'

◙ FROM SCHOOL TO COLLEGE ◙

'In 1939/40 as a very little girl I was taken by my aunt to see her sons at Weymouth College and although we only lived a few miles away, her sons boarded. Just inside the gateway of the school in Dorchester Road, there was a beautiful little chapel. The boys slept in huge dormitories with about 20 beds in each. They seemed very happy in school but starving! We took them fresh supplies for their tuck boxes and then we all went out for an enormous tea in a sea-front cafe. When the war got under way the school was evacuated and in their "new" school a Weymouth House was created. Sadly, they never came back to their own school. Instead, during the war the school was put to a variety of military and other uses.

After the war it became an Emergency Teacher Training College, where ex-servicemen and women received an intensive one-year training, which was essential as teachers were in very short supply and I understand that those teachers proved extremely good. The principal was a Miss O'Sullivan. When she retired in about 1949, Miss Maureen Weinstock took over and the college became a two-year teacher training college for women only. Under Miss Weinstock it rapidly grew, gained a fine reputation and the students were a familiar sight in Weymouth in their maroon blazers with woven wire badges (motto Tenare Cursum) and maroon and grey scarves.

Two large houses opposite the college were used to house the students and known as Budmouth and Casterbridge. The huge dormitories I had seen were still in use, but with fewer beds, as each student had a wardrobe and a desk/dressing-table/bookcase, plus a chair, as well as a bed. When Miss Weinstock retired, the college reverted to being one for mixed students; this would be about 1968. A new hostel was built, called Maiden Castle. Up until then some students had lived in various hotels in the town, where they had breakfast and evening meal – Netherton, at the bottom of Boot Hill was especially popular. Alas, in about 1987 the college closed as it was deemed too small. Weymouth had lost its boys' public school and Dorset its only teacher training college.'

◈ Nursing in the Workhouse ◈

'I got interested in nursing during a stay in the sanatorium and when a post for an orderly came up at the local workhouse at Wimborne I applied and was accepted. What an experience! I was in the hospital department but there was a place for the tramps who came for a night's sleep. All towns had a workhouse and they were nearly always a day's walk between. The tramps were given certain jobs to do before being allowed to leave in the morning.

A small church was on the premises and men sat one side and women the other and a local vicar took the services. Above the church there was a large room where before the war orphaned and illegitimate children could play. There was a handrail up the stairs for the adults and a little one further down for the children and seeing this little handrail always upset me.

In charge were a Master and Matron and we also had a Sister who was a midwife, who before the war had delivered the illegitimate babies in a small labour ward as many girls who were pregnant and unmarried were sent to the workhouse where they had to scrub floors and work before going into labour. One lady worked with the children, her husband had been gassed in the First World War so she had to work. One of her jobs was to take the babies for walks through the town in a long wicker pram, all dressed in identical clothes and known locally as the Union Bastards. How things have changed, thank goodness.

Many of our patients had been in the workhouse for over 50 years. As this was 50 years ago they were born 100 years ago and if born deformed no surgery was available as it is today, so there they stayed for the rest of their lives. From time to time we had to take our turn on night duty and I hated the night sister who I felt was very hard hearted with the patients. Between visiting the wards at half hourly intervals we sat in a room with a large Victorian fireplace and in the night the mice would come out from behind and we would feed them. There were also hundreds of cockroaches scuttling around especially near the old boiler.

In 1948 the Health Service commenced and I recall a lorry load of spring mattresses arriving as our patients were still using straw filled mattresses. They also brought linoleum for the floors, and curtains. This was wonderful and my main impression of the new Health Service.

The patients were treated by local GPs and I remember that if patients were on morphine we would put a tablet in a spoon with water and melt it over a bunsen burner; it was then drawn up into a glass syringe and Sister would inject it into the patient.'

▣ PADDLE STEAMERS AND LAUNDRY ▣

'One of my grandmothers worked on the paddle steamers that travelled between Weymouth and the Channel Islands; her husband was a sailor. My other grandmother was widowed when the eldest of her children was only 13 years old. Even when I was a child she still took in laundry. Sleeves rolled up and with plenty of water, she rubbed the washing on a scrubbing board and then all the garments were starched. She ironed with flat irons heated on the kitchen range.

My father was a builder by trade and at the start of his career he worked on many tall buildings, including the repairing of church spires and the building of the brewery chimney, and the repairing of the famous Hardy's Monument on Black Down. So that the renovation work did not show, dung and gravel were used. The wages in those days were very small and if the weather was inclement and the men could not work they did not get paid; there were certainly no paid holidays.'

▣ IN SERVICE ▣

'The school-leaving age in the 1930s was 14 and I chose to go into service. My first job was at a workmen's cafe, behind Butler's shop in

On the Weymouth paddle steamer to Jersey.

Withermoor Road, Bournemouth where I earned ten shillings a week. Two ladies ran the cafe and kept chickens and ducks in the garden behind. The work as a general domestic was very hard – scrubbing floors, preparing vegetables and endless washing-up – no washing-up liquid in those days, only washing soda and chapped hands. I got fed up with that after a while and went to another job, this time living-in at the golf club in Meyrick Park.

I had to start work at 5 am by scrubbing the clubroom out, ready for the golfers arriving at 6 am. The hours were very long and the atmosphere very depressing as the woman in charge was unfriendly. I felt so unhappy there, so on the fourth day I quietly packed my things in my basket, and while the boss was out at church during the morning, I sneaked out of the back door and ran as fast as I could over the golf-links for home. All I kept hearing was "Fore!" – it's a wonder nothing hit me. When I got home, my mother was very sympathetic.

I eventually went to work for a very nice Yorkshire lady in Wimborne Road and stayed there for nearly seven years. I was paid £3 a month which was quite good pay for a cook-general. The lady I worked for encouraged me to save so much each payday, so that when I got married at 24, I had saved £30. I had to buy my uniforms; in the mornings I wore a blue frock with a white cap and apron, while in the afternoons and evenings I wore a black frock with a white goffered cap and a white lace apron. Madam, as I called her, had a lovely flat on two floors in a big house with a beautiful garden and I looked after her, the flat and the garden all by myself.

We used to go out on trips to the countryside and to London, to the National Gallery and all sorts of other places. My time off was rather limited – only from 5 pm until 7 pm each day, a half day off each Wednesday and a half day on alternate Sundays. However, I was allowed to go to church at 7 am each Sunday. A whole day off was very rare – maybe an occasional bank holiday. After a half day out, I had to be back in by 10 pm. One day, my friend and I rode our bikes to Swanage. On the way back, we took a wrong turning at Wareham and finished up at Bere Regis. I was frantic with worry because I knew I would be late getting back. I could pedal faster than my friend so I had to leave her to race back on my own. I got back eventually at 10.30 pm, and happily didn't get a scolding as Madam was more concerned that I was all right.

I had a small bedroom up the back stairs, which was furnished with an iron bedstead with a flock mattress, a chest of drawers and a wash-stand plus a can for water for washing, which was obtained from the bathroom. Once, Madam had a friend to stay with his son, so I had to give up my bedroom for the son and move further into the attic. It was quite comfortable, with a little sash window, but probably quite a fire hazard when I think about it.

Madam was becoming more frail and decided to move to somewhere a little smaller, she left it to me to do the house-hunting. We decided on a house quite near, with a garden of course. At that time, I was 24 years old and had been courting for some time, so we decided to marry in 1939. Poor Madam was so upset, but she gave me a £10 cheque for a present. We left the area and didn't return for a few years. Some time later, I went to visit my old lady in a nursing home, and her funeral at Bournemouth crematorium was the first one I had ever been to. She did not forget me in her will, and I have nice pieces of silver and furniture to remind me of many happy days.'

'When I left school at 14 in 1945 I took a job as a mother's help for five shillings. Mum gave me sixpence pocket money. My next job paid 7s 6d. I got married in 1955 when my wages in domestic service were £2 10s. I borrowed a dress, but my veil, headdress and shoes were bought from my savings.'

'My mother, as a girl in the 1800s, worked as a maid at Weymouth. She was dismissed for wearing a pretty hat to church. Her mistress warned her, but she kept wearing it.'

▣ BRIDPORT AND MASS UNEMPLOYMENT ▣

'Fred Parsons recorded these memories of Bridport as it was at the turn of the century.

Sailing boats in Bridport Harbour.

"There are many things I remember about Bridport in the 1880s. I was born there in 1878 the son of a gardener, and the impressions of my early days are still as vivid as they were then. The Royal Artillery in their braided coats and spurs, when they marched out in the morning made a glittering parade of what we would look on nowadays as Ruritanian soldiers.

"There was mass unemployment in the town. My father had been brought up to gardening – and perhaps he left something of that in me – but at the time I remember he was working at Gundries Mill making fishing nets. This was because he had a family of four to keep, and the money there was better than he could make as a gardener. However, work got so bad that at last he was forced to leave there and return to his old trade. To relieve the unemployment a gentleman built the Esplanade down by the harbour, and men were employed cleaning the mud out of the pond at North Mills for no other reason than to give them work.

"Soup kitchens were opened, and you could buy half a pint of split pea soup for a penny. My mother would not let us go up to the soup kitchen, but would send me out for two pennyworth of bones instead, and make soup herself. To eke out Father's meagre wages, she would sit up late on Saturdays trimming ladies' hats for Sunday – she was a first-class needlewoman – but how she suffered from eyestrain, doing that intricate work by the light of an oil lamp. The poor couldn't afford glasses in those days, and I can see her now holding her aching head on Sunday mornings. But she kept the wolf from the door – we were always fed, if not sumptuously, at least adequately.

"New Zealand mutton was just being produced at that time, and was being sold at a stall opposite the market. No one would buy it, being suspicious of it, but it was the stall-holder's job to push it and what remained unsold at the end of the day would be sold by auction. I often saw a whole leg sold for a few pence. But it gradually got onto the market – and what a boon these auctions were to the poor, who often would have had no Sunday dinner at all but for them.

"I left school at the age of nine and went to work as a half-timer in a spinning works, turning the wheel while the old ladies spun the strands. We started at six o'clock in the morning. How I remember those cold, dark mornings, sitting on a wooden log turning the spinning wheel for the old men and women. I had to walk half a mile to work, and after dinner I went to school. My wages were 1s 6d a week. The sub-contractor was Mr Ackerman, and the works were halfway to West Allington."'

❖ BRIDPORT NETS ❖

'My father did 22 years of service in the Royal Navy and was away at the times that both my brother and I were born in the 1920s. It was quite often two and a half or three and a half years' service overseas then. Mothers rarely did full time jobs but if they needed to earn a bit of extra cash they would take in laundry from the people who were better off.

The net factories at Bridport also brought work to people's houses

Hanging the fishing nets, before the First World War.

at Abbotsbury. Some did "braiding", which meant making the big seine nets for fishing or nets for tennis courts or the little nets for the pockets of billiard tables. All were very hard work. The factories also sent out Brussels sprout nets already cut out for people to sew into bags; they were made from tarred string and smelled very strong. That was dirty work.'

▧ DORSET BUTTONS ▧

'When I first came to live in Twyford, in 1931, my husband bought two old cottages to make into our home. These were numbered 54 and 55, Twyford. On walking through the hamlet, which has neither church, shop, post office nor public house, I was amazed to find that there were only 14 or 15 cottages and a farm or two in the whole place. An old man lived nearby, and being of an enquiring type of mind, I asked him one day why my cottages had such numbers. He then told me that this had been a thriving village over a hundred years ago, when the button was being made by hand, and that when the trade declined, through the invention of the button machine, many families were starving; and that the government of the day had had them all deported, very unwillingly to Canada and Australia. He then took me round, showing me lilac, evergreen and other cultivated trees which appeared to be growing in the hedges of fields, and showed me "wild" gooseberry bushes, all of which in 1850 had been in the gardens of houses, but which were now the silent witnesses of a vanished community. I was so sorry for these long-dead victims of progress that I decided then and there to find out about this forgotten craft.

The history of the Dorset button began at Shaftesbury, probably between the years 1690 to 1700. Abraham Case made the first buttons which were known as "high tops" and from this lowly beginning came a trade which employed thousands in the county, men as well as women and children becoming proficient at the fine work. In its heyday, the trade brought in a revenue of £12,000 yearly (at a time when this meant a very large sum of money) and still might have been doing so if Ashton's button machine, invented in 1850, had not ruined the hand-made industry.

The Cases had depots all over Dorset and the neighbouring counties. Known depots were at Bere Regis, Milborne St Andrew, Blandford and Shaftesbury. Most of these depots remained in the hands of the Cases for well over a hundred years, and the depot of Milborne St Andrew until 1908 when the last surviving descendant of old Abraham died at the village post office.

From the first the buttons were actually made in the cottages and workhouses, stocks being brought by the workers to the various depots at fixed times. We are told that the towns resembled fairgrounds on Button Day and women thought little of walking a distance of ten miles to sell their wares. Button makers were seldom paid in cash, apparently, but in various goods, so that little could be put by for illness or old age. Blandford was busy with "buttony"; all in work-houses capable of holding and working a needle being put to the task. Thomas Bennett and Malachi Fisher were well known Blandford agents, as well as linen drapers. In 1905, Malachi Fisher's shop was sold and employees of the new firm were set to clear hundreds of boxes of hand-made buttons from the rear of the premises, and to burn them; these would be the stock in trade of the dealer, no doubt, when the machine-made article killed the market. Some of the girls retrieved a few cards and took them home, and the writer has a few of these.

In 1908, the Dowager Lady Lees bought the whole of the stock of buttons of old William Case on his death and tried to revive the industry at Lytchett Minster. She succeeded in building a small business, but the 1914–18 war killed it.'

WAR & PEACE

LOOKING BACK TO THE GREAT WAR

*M*emories *still remain among older Dorset folk of the days of the First World War, when the men left the towns and villages for the first time, many never to return. Oddly enough, it was often the little things that stayed in our minds – of German baths and Spanish mules.*

❖ SPANISH MULES ❖

'We lived in School Lane, Lulworth, opposite the smithy. There were thatched cottages where the brick houses are now, but they were burned down. The brick houses cost £90 each when they were built.

During the war the Army horses and mules were brought down from the camp at Newlands to be shod. Some of the mules were fresh from Spain and had never been shod. They had to be put in a wooden framework to control them.

Food was short during the war and we were glad to get hand-outs from the Army. I remember Ticklers jam in particular. There were four Italian prisoners of war on the farm and they got double rations.'

◼ GERMAN BATHS ◼

'My father built the house I still live in, during the First World War, at Langton Matravers. I was born in 1910 and one of the first things I remember about the house is having a bath in a proper bathroom. I would sit down and scream, "Get me out, this bath was made in Germany." I can only think that my brother must have said something to me about this.'

THE SECOND WORLD WAR 1939–1945

When the next war came, just over 20 years later, we were all in the front line and our lives changed overnight. Peaceful villages and seaside resorts suddenly found themselves at war, and things were never quite the same again.

◼ THE WAR IN BOURNEMOUTH ◼

'One terrible day was 23rd May 1943; it was a Sunday lunchtime, one o'clock. My baby daughter was just two months old, asleep in her pram in the garden. The Germans dropped bombs on the Hotel Metropole at the Lansdowne, opposite the Municipal College and killed a lot of Canadian soldiers who were having a lunchtime drink at the bar. Another bomb fell on the London Hotel at the bottom of Richmond Hill, and killed more Canadian and American soldiers there. Beale's (the big shop in Bournemouth) and the Punchon Memorial church, which was then on Richmond Hill, were utterly destroyed. The church of the Sacred Heart, also on Richmond Hill, and many other shops and churches were badly damaged. Fortunately, it being a Sunday morning the shops were shut and the church services were over, otherwise the loss of life would have been dreadful: 53 people altogether were killed on that day. We saw all the debris go up from our house in Burton. Another bomb fell on the gas depot at Branksome and killed a lot of young gas workers there, in their canteen at lunchtime. My sister and a friend were walking along Beechey Road in Bournemouth and they actually saw the German planes go over and saw the pilots in their planes and they had nowhere to take cover.

Near my old home in Portland Road in Winton, houses were badly damaged and in another road people were killed. My parents' house was the last one not touched and my mother gave shelter to neighbours all night and made cups of tea for them. No one had an air raid shelter as the government never thought places like Bournemouth would be bombed.

A huge landmine fell on my old school in Alma Road which I attended in my primary days. Our old home in Kings Road at the back of the school and several other houses were destroyed. Our old home has never been rebuilt, there is only a green mound there.

My husband's boss and his wife were machine-gunned by a German plane as they walked from Bournemouth pier across to the Pleasure Gardens one Sunday morning.

There were many Americans billeted in the hotels around Bournemouth during the war and the Bournemouth girls went mad over them as they looked so smart compared with our Tommies and they always seemed to have plenty of money, sweets and best of all, silk stockings, when all we English had was lisle or wool stockings. Many of the Bournemouth girls married Yanks. Some of the English girls were told that Daddy had a ranch in the USA, but when they got to America after the war they were often no more than huts.

The Germans had a big store of bombs in Cherbourg, which is only 60 miles from Bournemouth. Fortunately the RAF destroyed the bombs, otherwise Bournemouth would have been wiped out. The Germans had chosen Bournemouth to be the headquarters for printing their own currency and it was to be an important place for them after the war.

I very well remember after Dunkirk, waiting at the Triangle in Bournemouth when I saw hundreds of French soldiers who had just arrived by train at the old Bournemouth West station. They were being taken to the schools all around the town. They had been rescued by the little boats like our own lads. I couldn't make out what it was all about. They were very dirty and ragged. My Guide Captain got together other Guides and the WVS etc and they bathed their feet and washed their hands and faces. It must have been her last good turn before she was killed. She sent out a message for people to give socks, underclothes, shirts etc for the French soldiers to replace their dirty torn ones. My mother and I fished out all my dad's and husband's old socks and underclothes and darned and mended them and gave them to her. Remember clothes were rationed then. People gave their scarce food as well. These French soldiers joined the Free French troops under General de Gaulle, who afterwards became President of France.

During the war Bournemouth and Boscombe piers were blown up and there were iron defences built in the sea, all along Bournemouth seafront from Hengistbury Head to Mudeford and to Sandbanks, to keep the Germans from landing. You could not swim, but you could paddle.'

❖ ALWAYS PEOPLE STAYING ❖

'We had evacuee children from Southampton billeted in Portesham in 1940; one teacher came with them so the school was somewhat crowded and some old fashioned desks that were in the playground were used, which had no backs to the seats. There was no air raid shelter so when the siren sounded we sat around the stairs and hall in the school house.

The first year I was at the technical college we spent a lot of time in the shelters, but this was stopped and we only went down there when they thought there was real danger. Teachers did not seem to stay long as there was a shortage of trained ones. Those who stayed were quite often of retirement age. At home we always seemed to have people staying, evacuees (a granny, her grandson and granddaughter), or soldiers' wives who had come to the area to visit their husbands, one lady I still hear from. Homework was either done on

At Maumbury Rings, Dorchester.

the train home, or on a corner of the kitchen table, trying to get the best light from the oil lamp, because if someone wanted to read they would try and get the lamp near them.

Until 1950 all milking of cows was by hand and my mother often went to help when the men were busy or short of milkers. We made just enough butter for ourselves, a Guernsey cow being specially kept for this; when she was dry the butter and milk were not the same. We always had chickens and quite often ducks as well, so apart from sugar and tea rationing during the war we were not affected too badly. Dad grew all his own vegetables and potatoes.

I started work in the printers in 1943, so was in Weymouth and saw the preparations for D-Day: the build-up of forces, the Allied sailors who came ashore, most of all the Americans. The bakery next to our works was taken over by Americans, and our apprentices used to go and get cream cakes, the likes of which we hadn't seen for years. Across the road was an officers' club, where they seemed to be all day. I suppose it was different ones on days off. A lot of Weymouth, around the harbour, was "out of bounds", Alexandra Gardens became HMS *Grasshopper*, and the Pavilion and ballroom were taken over by the Navy. Just before D-Day the Americans took over the Royal Hotel and in the mornings when one went from the station to the office, the US officers would be sat in the entrance drinking coffee. In spite of all the forces in Weymouth we weren't afraid of walking to the station in the blackout, on our own.

The only scare I had was on Wednesday night, cycling from the station home to the farm. Bicycles were only allowed very small lights and there being no other traffic, one virtually went along in the middle of the road. At a bend at the end of the village, a black figure came into view. It started screaming. I pedalled home like mad, then afterwards I realised *I* had frightened *him*. Next day Mum went to the village and heard about the six foot black US soldier who had been frightened by a banshee; he had been away from his billet and hearing the train knew he was late and was hurrying back.'

▣ A Terrible Night ▣

'On Good Friday, 1941 bombs were dropped in the valley at Toller Fratrum. They were intended for the searchlight unit. The blast shattered all the metal and plate glass windows in the house and church, but the cottages escaped. It was a terrible, terrible night, never will I forget it. The Home Guard unit thought we were no more.'

▣ Soldiers in Abbotsbury ▣

'When war broke out in 1939 my father was called back into the Navy and he was sent to sea on an old fishing boat which was used for mine-sweeping. He was there for a few months but contracted lung trouble and was invalided out of the services, then my brother was called up into the Army.

After the fall of Dunkirk in 1940 we had soldiers billeted in the village. Empty houses and spare rooms were requisitioned, tents were put up anywhere as long as they were out of sight from the air. Nissen huts were built in several places on the outskirts of the village.

Every three or four months, one regiment would move out and another one move in.

The blackout was awful, all the windows had to be blacked out, not a bit of light had to show through anywhere. You couldn't use a torch in the streets. We still had oil lamps and candles. The electric had just been brought to Abbotsbury but when war broke out all that work stopped. I think it was about 1948 by the time our house was wired.

In 1943 British troops moved out of the area and the Americans came to our villages. They were very friendly with the village people and on Boxing Day they invited quite a few villagers to a party at the camp. There was no shortage of anything. We hadn't seen tinned peaches or chocolate biscuits all through the war years, but they had everything on the menu. That was the first time I tasted sweetcorn, not one of my favourite things.

The Americans came to this area for the build up of troops for the invasion of Europe. Thousands passed through Portesham and embarked from Weymouth and Portland. After the troops left the villages returned to normal everyday life. When the war finished bonfires were lit and there was dancing in the streets all night. Village people know how to enjoy themselves when they feel inclined. It all seems an awful long time ago.'

▩ BARBED WIRE AT SWANAGE ▩

'During the war most of the guest houses at Swanage were used to billet servicemen, and later for the American forces. Barbed wire and iron girders were put all along the beaches and coastline, and after the war German prisoners of war had to be drafted in to make it safe.'

▩ GETTING WED ▩

'Leaving Moreton school at 14 years old, I went into service in the big house owned by Lord and Lady Duff. I was there for six years, and when the war broke out the Air Force took over the property.

There was an airfield in Crossways and that was how I met my

All arranged in one week – a wartime wedding at Crossways.

husband to be, who was in the first squadron to move into the area. He, of course, moved around the country and one day in 1941 he notified me he was having a week's leave and we could get married. I begged and borrowed coupons and went to the store in Dorchester and managed to purchase a wedding dress and also ordered a wedding cake. This was all done on the Monday and we were married on the Friday in the little chapel at Crossways.'

DOING OUR BIT

Whether in the Home Guard or the Women's Land Army, we all did our bit for the war effort. With the influx of soldiers into the area, entertaining the troops was an important job for local people.

IN THE HOME GUARD

'At Alderholt 32 men were recruited into the Local Defence Volunteers, later to be called the Home Guard. The platoon headquarters were in the old village hall, and guards were posted each night at the railway bridge at the station. One volunteer remembers being on duty with a red lantern, supposedly stopping all vehicles. Instead he was talking to a pal, and when a car passed him he grabbed his rifle and fired, luckily missing the car. The owner turned out to be a British army officer coming home on leave.

During the war several bombs were dropped in Alderholt, and in 1942 a Heinkel III bomber was shot down; some of the crew bailed out nearby and were captured.'

THE WEYMOUTH BW CANTEEN

'On Saturday, 5th October 1940, Captain and Mrs King opened the BW Canteen for servicemen and women in Weymouth. BW was short

Bridport ATC in 1941.

for the National British Women's Total Abstinence Union and anyone coming into the club smelling of alcohol was quietly taken aside and severely lectured on the evils of drink by Mrs King! I became a voluntary helper almost as soon as the club opened, my mother joining later on. My mother would leave to get the last bus home, but I stayed until the club closed, walking a good two miles, including through the centre of Weymouth in the blackout. Weymouth was bursting at the seams with troops of all nationalities and yet I was never afraid of any unpleasantness.

A cup of tea at the club was 1d, Cornish pasties, vegetable pies, bacon and egg pies (made with reconstituted eggs) were 4d, sausage and mash, or fried spam and bread were 6d. Among the desserts was the BW pudding made from soaked stale bread, flour, suet, spice and as much dried fruit as possible, mixed with treacle and milk and baked in a large tin. Any leftovers were sold at 1d a lump. Lentil soup was 2d, a large mug was appreciated on cold nights. All the cooking and baking was done on the premises by volunteers. (My memory of the prices was refreshed by Mrs King's *Happy Recollections*.)

Sometimes there would be a pianist amongst the boys and girls and we would be treated to everything from the classics to a roof raising sing-song.

At one Christmas party a game of forfeits was organised. There couldn't have been many young helpers there that evening for the soldier who had to kiss the prettiest girl as his forfeit chose me. I expected a peck on the cheek but I found myself crushed to his manly khaki-clad chest, being thoroughly kissed. Mrs King, I heard later, turned to my mother and enquired "Does your daughter know that young man?" I was terribly shocked when Mother replied, "I don't think so." The outcome was that from then on kissing games were banned!

On the last evening of November 1943 the blackout was pushed aside and into the club walked the first two GIs we had ever seen. They had arrived in Dorset the night before after campaigns in Sicily and North Africa and been given weekend leave. Most had gone up to London, but these two came into Weymouth, found somewhere to stay for the night, then set off to find some entertainment. After wandering around in the blackout they heard music and singing and decided to investigate. Somewhat taken aback at finding the room full of British troops they nevertheless ventured in, and were soon sitting drinking their first cup of English tea.

The result of this was that the following May I became a GI bride, married for just three weeks when my husband left Weymouth for the Omaha beach in Normandy on D-Day.

In February of that year the Americans had opened their own Forces Club in the town, so we didn't have many American visitors to the BW Club. Often there would be dances at the American Club with a great dance band in which Bob played the trombone, I would always go along as a guest. It was great fun.

On VE Day I went to the BW club in the morning with my husband on his first leave since D-Day and took 20 small bunches of red, white and blue flowers which my mother had picked from our garden. They looked so bright and patriotic on the tables.

I continued helping at the club until it closed in September 1945, which was a very emotional occasion, especially for those of us who had helped all the time the club was open.'

▨ A Bit of a Shock ▨

'I remember the shock I had when I joined the Land Army and was sent to Portesham. Living in Blackpool, I had grown up with all mod cons and to be presented with a bowl of water to "wash up as far as possible and down as far as possible", and to go down the garden to the "privy" – well! Still, I was young then and life was fun so it didn't worry me for long.'

▨ Helping with the Deliveries ▨

'I was 16½ in January 1942. I was a butcher's daughter and my wartime job was delivering the very small meat rations to our customers in the country.

The time was about 6.30 pm, pitch dark and snowing. I had to walk down a hill to deliver meat to a farmhouse at Corton, between Portesham and Coryates. My driver, the butcher, left me to drive to Higher Friar Waddon, a farm towards Martinstown, right out in the wilds. He told me, "I won't be long, wait for me at the gate across the road." As the fields were open, this gate was the boundary between the farm of Friar Waddon and Corton. I was scared stiff of cows, and in those days they had *horns*. I stood there with my little torch, and waited and waited. Finally, it seemed like hours and hours, my driver and his van appeared. The snow was thicker by then and the farmer had had to help him dig out the van. I was never so thankful to see anybody in my life, the cows were all round me, both sides of the gate.'

A CHILD'S WAR

Children faced terrors of their own, from evacuation to their fears of air raids and gas masks. Evacuation in particular could prove a trial, but many friendships were made and, somehow, schooling went on.

▨ EVACUEES AND SIRENS ▨

'When the war started we had a flood of evacuees in Dorchester. They were in a very poor state and many had their heads shaved, but they soon settled in.

When the air raid sirens went we had to form orderly lines with our gas masks over our shoulders and walk about three minutes up the road to a field where trenches were dug for us to shelter in. As it became apparent that we were quite safe in Dorchester we ceased to go to the trenches. One very vivid war memory was when the troops flooded the town when they returned from Dunkirk – they were everywhere, sleeping wherever they could find a spot to rest their weary bodies.

I did not get the opportunity to go to the girls' grammar school but I did go to the newly built secondary modern school for boys and girls. We had wonderful facilities, including a gymnasium and shower cubicles, which were compulsory after any games or physical exercise (if you did not want to shower you had to report to the headmaster). The boys played cricket and football and the girls netball and hockey. As the school was new and took in children from the surrounding villages, there was an IQ test for all pupils, all sitting in the large hall. There were three streams for each school year. The arrival of evacuees also brought teachers from London; these were all very good. I left school just before my 14th birthday and went straight into a large grocery store in the accounts department; the shop supplied all the army camps in the area.'

▩ EVACUATED TO DORSET ▩

'I came to Dorset in 1940, evacuated from London with my brother and mother on the mothers and children scheme. My father followed later after our house in London was demolished by a bomb.

We moved into a farm cottage which had been empty for two years. It was pretty damp. The wallpaper had been nailed up! Anyway, we could have this treasure on condition that we housed and cared for three boy evacuees from Southampton.

This cottage had three bedrooms and two rooms downstairs, but the back bedroom was over the woodshed which made it very draughty, the lino rising up when the wind blew.

The four boys occupied this room, it quite easily housed four single beds. Electricity was laid on, but water was from a "stick well". This well was about eight yards from the front (and only) door; you had to hook the bucket on the long stick (like a clothes prop) with a crook on the end, push the bucket under the water and capture the handle when the bucket was full and pull up. We took quite a time to

179

get used to this, and had to fish many a bucket out with grappling irons. All water used was carried in via the front door, which led straight into the living room, and all water taken out by the same route.

This made bath night quite a performance. The zinc bath was placed in front of the old blackleaded range, with the clothes horse around for a little privacy! When we bathed the boys, my mother washed and I dried, with stops to take some of the water out and add some hot water. Never a complete change of water.

The garden was quite large and grew some super vegetables. The "loo" was of the bucket type so it was a good job we had a large garden! For this desirable residence the rent was five shillings a week and this included rates.

Quite often we would have rabbit for dinner. My father had to learn to skin these carefully, head as well, then peg them out on a board. Every so often a man came and collected these skins and paid sixpence for them.'

▨ MASS EVACUATION AND BOMBS ▨

'I remember the day war was declared very vividly. I went to church for morning service, and a wireless had been brought in so that we could hear Mr Neville Chamberlain's statement. Mass evacuation from London had been arranged for that day, of school children and mothers with young children and babies. Bridport grammar school (at which I was a pupil) was just near the railway station and was to be the reception centre. From before lunch until 10 pm trains continually arrived, and tea and currant buns were supplied to all by a team of helpers, of whom my mother and I were two. It was quite an eye-opener for me, a mere 13 year old, seeing all these people, some from the slums of London, mothers breast-feeding their babies outside in public.

During the Battle of Britain, 1940, it was quite usual to pick up spent bullets when shopping in the town. We watched dog-fights between our own and German fighters in the skies above us, and one

The American Red Cross canteen at Bridport, converted from the old Scientific and Literary Institute.

Hurricane had engine trouble and force-landed in one of my father's fields outside Shipton Gorge.

We had bombs dropped on Bridport. The first came on a summer Sunday, early evening, and I was upstairs in my second-floor bedroom, sitting near the window and writing a letter. I looked up to see these two fighter-bombers coming in over the town from the Burton Bradstock direction, and the bombs were falling from the planes, dropping in the main street of the town. Many of the windows on the front of the house were shattered by the blast. When we had the second raid, just before Christmas of 1942, one of the bombs dropped was wedged in the doorpost of the Westminster Bank, but it did not go off. Arrangements were made for many of the inhabitants of East Street to be evacuated, but this was not necessary as men of a Bomb Disposal Unit came and fortunately removed it intact.

Throughout the war troops were billeted in Bridport. During 1942 the beaches of the district were used as practice points for the Canadian Army, prior to the unfortunate landing at Dieppe. In the autumn of 1943 the Americans arrived. They were of the First Infantry Division, and had already taken part in the North African landing and the Anzio beach-head in Italy. They prepared, of course, for D-Day, including a dummy run on the coast of North Devon. The Scientific and Literary Institute in East Street, Bridport (now the library) was converted into an American Red Cross canteen. A very gifted illustrator billeted locally painted some cartoons on the canteen walls to make the rooms look more "interesting".

As D-Day approached, more and more soldiers seemed to come to the area. It was a regular thing to have large troop-carrying vehicles and tanks parked nose-to-tail along the sides of the roads. On one occasion, to my acute embarrassment, when I was driving to Dorchester, along the road in front of Poundbury Farm, I came upon such a column, stationary, on the right-hand side of the road. There was traffic coming against me and, in addition, on the left-hand side was a long column of GIs marching towards me, four abreast. I could do nothing but stop and sit tight, with the column splitting in front of me, two going on each side.'

▨ WE ALL GOT ON ▨

'My brother joined the Navy, Father the ARP. Mother took in three evacuees, two boys and one girl. I was just eleven then. We all got on fine. Things had not changed in the way of water, lavatory and cooking, so it must have been pretty awful for them coming from London.

We all attended Woodville Stour Provost school, where two classrooms were made into four. Heating was by combustion stoves, the lavatories were outside, with one old washbasin (cold water) in the lobby with all our coats. We took sandwiches for lunch, or could walk home if there was enough time. Miss Carter, the headmistress, was strict but nice; Miss Kenward the London teacher was very lenient. We had our own choices of class work (it was arithmetic we chose).

We used to help the ARP wardens with their practices, and we went on farms planting potatoes. There was a Forces hospital near us (Guys Marsh, now a Borstal) and the girls used to darn a lot of their socks (horrible job).

I left school at 14 and started work in 1943. A lot of evacuees went home. One boy stayed with us until the end of the war, he loved it here and still does. I keep in contact with all three.

We did have a few bombs dropped round here, 17 one night, you could hear them whistling down. We were downstairs under the table and blanket. Father was on duty.'

▨ YOU ARE MY SUNSHINE ▨

'You are my sunshine
My only sunshine
You make me happy
When skies are grey . . .

So sang the children of Oakdale council school, Poole, in 1940, squashed together on wooden benches, deep underground. Singing lustily, we leaned back against dripping earth walls studded with fungi. Stagnant water seeped beneath the slatted floorboards. Later they built replacement brick shelters above ground on land behind the school.

Once I remember a spine-chilling rumour circulating about a fatal parachute jump when the parachute became entangled in the aircraft door. The pilot flew low over Poole Harbour for the drop.

We were in deep trouble if we forgot to bring our gas masks to school. Gruesome warnings made us shiver about being blown to pieces should we pick up suspicious objects lying among the heather on the heathlands like Canford Heath. For a short time we shared our lesson time with evacuees from Southampton, and took turn and turn about to attend either morning or afternoon school.

We were warned, also, always to wait for the air raid wardens to blow whistles and shout "Raiders past", before emerging from air raid shelters after the all clear siren sounded. When I was nine, in 1940, we shared an underground Anderson shelter with neighbours. The boy who lived in the road behind took pleasure in emerging from his shelter on the first note of the all clear. Sadly, he was killed by bomb blast in October 1940.

This was the night before I was whisked off to Alderney isolation hospital with scarlet fever. Nurse Rose, who came with me in the ambulance, raised me up to look out of the window at the bomb damage not realising that because we lived in a cul de sac our bungalow almost backed on to the missing ones. During my four weeks' stay in hospital I saw a German aircraft crash a quarter of a mile away. A landmine dropped in the vicinity and caused some indirect damage to our ward, the wall on one side parting from the floor.

After this I was happy to return to school. There were good things to remember about my schooldays too. One of them was winning prizes, not for academic prowess but for collecting the most salvage. I can still smell the hessian sandbags issued for the weekly house-to-house collection of newspapers to be carted to school next day to be weighed. I also won the prize for killing the most cabbage white butterflies which threatened the war effort of growing for victory, but like to keep *that* quiet in these conservation-minded times!

Oakdale school today looks much the same from the outside as it did all those years ago when we marched out of it to take shelter. If ever I hear a certain evocative tune now I am instantly back in those dank underground passages singing:

You'll never know dear,
How much I love you.
Please don't take my sunshine away.'

▩ FREEDOM IN SPITE OF THE WAR ▩

'Looking back on my childhood I realise the freedom we had in spite of the war. We wandered the fields and woods picking the wild flowers for Mum, and in general learning about the countryside. We had picnics on Castle Hill, often walked to Melbury Hill, and spent many hours in Motcombe and Coombe woods, but we knew it was one o'clock dinner, five o'clock tea and on summer evenings eight o'clock we had to be home. We carried no keys as Mum was always there, most of her life spent cooking, washing and cleaning.

I WISH TO MARK, BY THIS PERSONAL MESSAGE, my appreciation of the service you have rendered to your Country in 1939.

In the early days of the War you opened your door to strangers who were in need of shelter, & offered to share your home with them.

I know that to this unselfish task you have sacrificed much of your own comfort, & that it could not have been achieved without the loyal co-operation of all in your household.

By your sympathy you have earned the gratitude of those to whom you have shown hospitality, & by your readiness to serve you have helped the State in a work of great value.

Elizabeth R

Mrs. Seymour.

A message of thanks to those who gave shelter to evacuees.

I remember standing in the garden watching the gliders being towed by planes, and we could hear the sound of tanks coming down the Grosvenor Road, so we would make a dash to the town to see if we could get some gum if it was the Americans. How they missed the houses on the corner we will never know. Two evacuees arrived at our house, one bringing her headlice with her. The special comb for this purpose was used every night, and it was quite a stigma if it was known you had nits. The hair was cut short and shingled at the back. I lived in fear of this, but managed to stay with just the "pudding basin cut" as they called it. We also had a Commando stay for two to three weeks, who slipped off somewhere never to be heard of again.

My dad, as well as being a butcher, was a special constable during the war. His remark as the first siren went was, "Where's my whistle and tin hat!", and off he went, leaving my mother and myself and one cat and dog to fend for ourselves. I think he spent most of his time going round shouting, "Put that light out", when we did not close the blackout just right.'

A Village at War

V erwood, a village in the east of the county, faced the same problems we all did, and the villagers' recollections are a reminder of the trials and tribulations of life at war.

'The Second World War made a greater impact on the life of the village than anything before or since. Everyone in the village knew everyone else, and yet in the war years people were to take in evacuees, to find soldiers, both British and American, billeted upon them and prisoners of war, both German and Italian, working in their fields. Young men from the village fought on land, at sea and in the air. The Dorset Regiment was at Arnhem. One Verwood man

A jam making centre organised at Verwood produced 340 lbs of jam in 1941, but in 1942 this was surpassed by an almost unbelievable 2,000 lbs!

brought prisoners of war back from France after D-Day. A landing craft was used and he remembers boat load after boat load of seasick Germans landed at various points along the coast to be taken inland to camps. Another young man drove a supply lorry across France and Germany to Berlin. At least one man from the village became a "Bevin boy"; a number of women joined either the Services or the Land Army, others stayed behind to run farms and businesses. All played their part in some way.

At home there were the upheavals of air raids and a multitude of minor upsets. The blackout was a continual nightmare. Even the smallest chink of light from windows called forth recriminations. There is a story of an unpopular warden who went into the Punch and Judy Cafe next to St Raphael's in Manor Road and complained that the Germans could see the light from their gas rings. Heated words ensued and after the warden was pulled through the hedge a constable was called to restore the peace.

Cars, such as were on the roads, drove with their headlights masked with just a narrow strip for the light to shine through to see and be seen. Obviously even those streets which were lit in the normal way were blacked out and, for the first few months, torches were not allowed. One lady remembers cycling home when the oil lamp on her bicycle caught alight and she had to jump into a ditch for safety.

In October 1939 the vicar of St Michael's suggested the church should be fitted with screens at the top of the windows and curtains below. However, in December it was decided that lights should be lowered and shades put over them, but in September 1941 the time of Evensong was brought forward three and a half hours to 3.30 pm. This not only eased the lighting problem but also allowed parishioners to get home before dark. The school hours had already been amended to 9.15 to 12.15 and 1.45 to 3.45 pm.

Because of troop movements and the transport of war material, train travel was very difficult with trains being very crowded, often delayed by bombings on the line and darkened carriages and stations. At this time children from the village attended secondary schools in Parkstone or Wimborne. One lady, then aged eleven, remembers the trains often stopping on the line between Verwood and Poole with long unexplained waits. On one occasion it could not enter Poole and had to return. On another, she remembers being unable to get home because of delays on the line and having to stay overnight with friends.

A further hazard was added after Dunkirk when all station names were removed and signposts taken down to impede the enemy. At this time all vehicles had to be immobilised when left – this usually entailed the removal of the rotor arm.

Few people had shelters. One family who had a trench said they didn't use it as they were too interested in what was happening. Another family recall sleeping on the ground floor and watching the mice run round them. Most adults took part in firewatching.

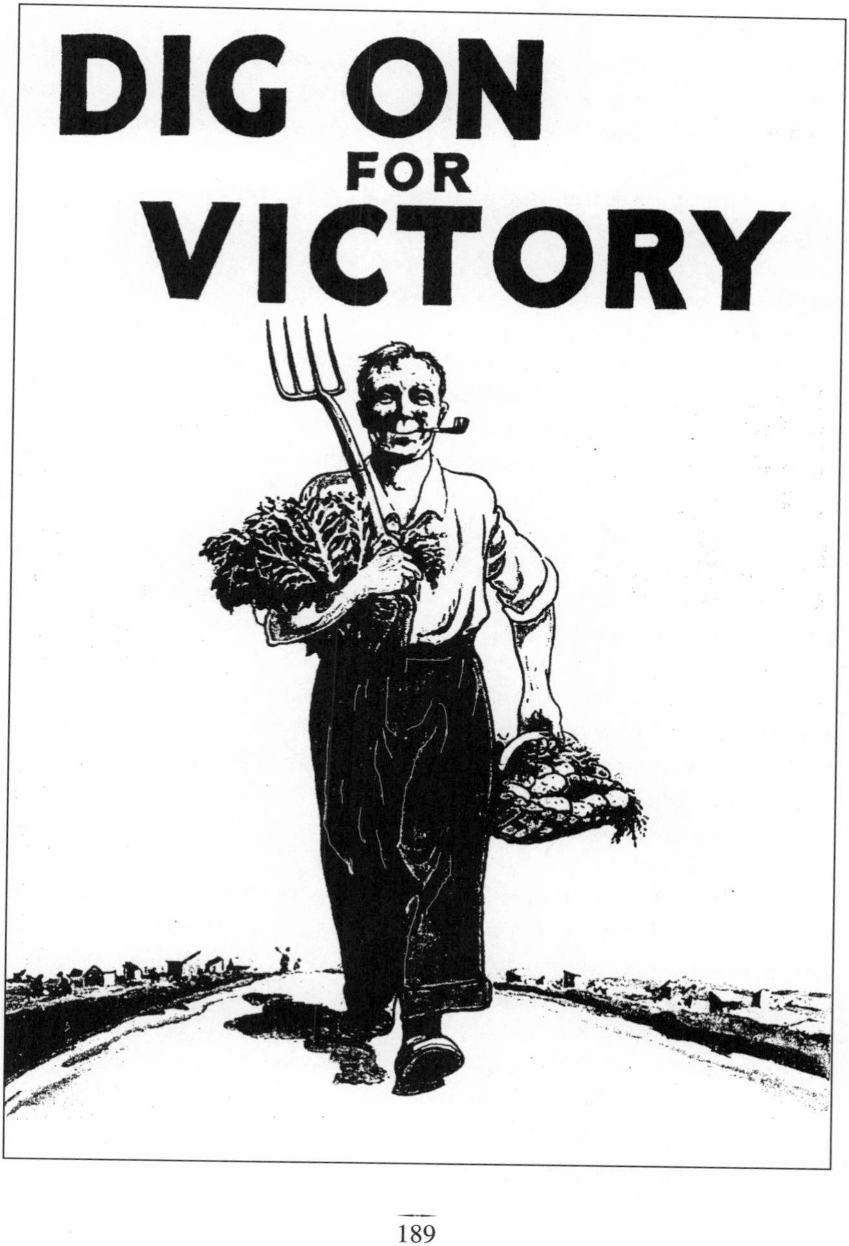
DIG ON
FOR
VICTORY

Among some of the trivial inconveniences of life at this time was the difficulty of getting presents for the bran tub at the annual church Christmas fete and the fact that the military had commandeered the trestle tables normally used. The following Christmas, concern was expressed in the church committee minutes about what stalls could be arranged in view of the difficulty caused by the rationing of so many articles.

Posters everywhere warned people that "careless talk costs lives". Another poster which displeased some people and so was quickly withdrawn begged readers to "Be like Dad, keep Mum".

When clothes rationing began in 1941 things became even more difficult. Each person had 48 coupons per month to use on all clothing including footwear. This made replacement very difficult and, in July 1944 the WI sold leather patches presumably for the elbows and possibly cuffs.

In 1942 Mr George Bailey, the barber, was called up for the Navy, a corner of a garage was curtained off and Mr Shearing cut the men's hair. However, if a customer came in with a punctured tyre the poor man was left half shorn until the repair was completed.

In contrast to all the gloom, many morale boosters were organised. There was the occasional "hop" at Ringwood or Cranborne and the WI Old Folks teas carried on although transport caused problems due to shortage of petrol. At least some of the money raised for war charities was the profit from card parties, socials and garden fetes. Moreover, most people derived great satisfaction from "doing their bit".

Empire Day and Armistice Day were celebrated as they always had been. The former was traditionally a half-holiday from school but on at least two occasions during the war years the teachers took the children out for a picnic and ramble on that day. Sports Day was, as now, an important day in the school year. The sports were organised by the teachers and an excerpt in the Verwood council school log book reads: "On 16.9.44 the Home Guard No 3 platoon led by Lieut Bates and Plt Sergt H.C. Barrow provided the means and prizes (£20 12s 3d) for a Children's Sports day today."

Newcomers to the village also added a whole new outlook. Apart from the Service personnel, there were land girls, one of whom married a farm worker in the village, Italian prisoners of war doing ditching and German POWs working on the farms.

From quite early in the war there were soldiers in the village. They were expected at the beginning of October 1939 and the WI could not hold their meeting in the usual place, "the hall having been commandeered for the soldiers who did not come".

However, it wasn't long before they did arrive and were billeted in the village hall and joined in the life of the village. One man regularly went along to the barber's shop on Saturdays and helped by sharpening his razors for the Saturday Shaving Day, and those villagers who were lucky enough to have bathrooms allowed the men to use them.

By June 1940 the Toc H had been taken over by the Military and there was a searchlight detachment in Woodlands and at least one in Verwood itself.

Soldiers returning from Dunkirk came through the village, the old village hall being used as a canteen for them. Troop trains travelled through the station to Weymouth, cordite coming from Horton Common and tanks and army vehicles from Blandford going through the village. On one occasion the track came off a tank near the crossroads and landed in the front garden of a house in Station Road.

In April 1942 the County Secretary of the WI asked members to give hospitality to Canadian soldiers in the country but there is no record of them arriving in the village. On the other hand, the arrival of the Americans made a great impact here. Literally, in the case of a schoolboy who was knocked over by a truck near the entrance to the market in Manor Road. The Corporal concerned was based in West Moors but living in "The Albion" in Verwood.

In April 1939 the Wimborne and Cranborne Rural District Council told West Moors to expect 2,100 children from Portsmouth to be billeted in the area. In the first place householders were asked to put a card in their window if they were prepared to participate in the scheme. Apparently this did not produce results so, in Verwood, Miss Limpus called on people asking for their help. Mrs Coombes said, "I'll have to if it'll help", and had one evacuee aged six until he left school. Her son, Mervyn, had a parcel with 6d enclosed from the boy's mother who sometimes visited the child, described as a "townie teara-way". However, although throughout the country and even other parts of Dorset there were many stories of destruction and havoc caused by evacuees there were few in Verwood.

Attached to trees, lampposts and pillar boxes were yellow strips which would change colour in the presence of mustard gas. For a very long time everyone carried their gas masks with them wherever they went.

In Verwood there was no siren although one was asked for on several occasions. On 15th October 1940 the head ARP warden wrote to the Wimborne RDC to say that: "...the present system of warning by messenger in this parish is totally inadequate having regard to the nature and size of the parish..." As late as July 1944 over 300 villagers petitioned for a siren but it was still refused. Instead, when the red alert was received by the ARP and First Aid Post at the Restynge House, the wardens cycled round the village blowing short blasts on their whistles. When the all clear was received the process was repeated but this time long blasts were sounded. Had there been a gas warning, rattles would have been used.

It is not surprising, bearing in mind the number of air raids suffered by the village, that a warden's bicycle tyre wore out and he applied to the council for 10s towards the cost of a new one. Nor is it surprising that his request was turned down.

The first occasion upon which bombs were dropped on the village was 1st July 1940. When the District Officer phoned to give Verwood the red alert his conversation was interrupted by the failure of all telephones. So he set out in his car to pass on the warning. When he reached Three Legged Cross he found bombs had already fallen although the signalman had heard nothing. He got in touch with the line foreman and stopped all trains. In the event it proved that 15 bombs were dropped at intervals of 150 yards in a line running from south to north parallel with the railway between Three Legged Cross and Verwood. Two did not explode and of the remainder most fell on

A Verwood land girl.

open heathland causing little damage. Three, however, fell near houses at Three Legged Cross and broke windows and roof tiles and damaged surface brickwork. In one or two cases splinters penetrated walls of the houses and were found scattered about inside. A greenhouse and fowl houses were demolished and the poultry killed. Through all this there was only one minor human casualty – a lady at Three Legged Cross who jumped out of bed onto a red-hot bomb splinter.

Throughout the next four years there were innumerable alerts as the bombers passed over the village on their way to Bristol, the Midlands or Southampton and high explosive and incendiary bombs were dropped on several occasions. There were a number of unexploded bombs, which in some cases necessitated people from nearby houses being evacuated until the bomb could be dealt with.

On one occasion a suspicious hole appeared although no one had heard a bomb drop nor were there the tell-tale splinters or any blacking round the hole. Nevertheless, the matter was dealt with in the usual way and the area roped off until the bomb disposal team could arrive a few days later to deal with it – only to find that the hole was caused by natural subsidence; an example of better safe than sorry.

In all, with one exception, these raids caused more nuisance than damage. The exception was on 24th April 1944. By this time it was obvious to everyone – German as well as English – that the "Second Front" was imminent. It was also obvious that large troop concentrations would take place along the South Coast. So, on 24th April 1944 the whole of Dorset received the red alert and most of the county suffered damage. It was, no doubt, an educated guess that equipment would be concealed in the forest and so Verwood had its heaviest raid of the war.

On 8th May 1945 Verwood council school assembled as usual at 9 am and a Thanksgiving Service of praise and song was held. The headmaster gave an address. Milk was served and then all adjourned to the recreation ground where the field was laid out for sports in the evening. The children were dismissed at 12 noon. Sports organised by the teachers and funded by public subscription through the parish council were run from 4 pm to 7 pm.

The main celebrations did not take place until 8th June when, because of rain, the sports programme was cancelled. Nevertheless, all the children of Verwood and Three Legged Cross assembled in the Verwood council school and were entertained to songs, tea, lemonade, milk and ice cream. The chairman of the parish council, Mr Barrow addressed the children.

It may be wondered why, with victory over Japan still three months away and austerity to become worse before rationing ceased in the mid 1950s, the village should rejoice so wholeheartedly in 1945. For six years everyone had been living a completely unnatural life. Although the actual number of bombs dropped in the village was small, night after night the alert would sound and people would get up and go to their "shelter" never knowing whether the bombers were passing on their way to Bristol, Southampton or the Midlands or whether it was "our turn tonight". For years the ARP and Home Guard had been on duty night after night in good weather or bad and still carried out their normal work during the day. Most adults had done some form of war work and fortunate was the child who did not suffer in some way or other. Now everyone could be assured of a good night's sleep knowing they did not stand the chance of being bombed in bed. There had been the continual worry about loved ones serving in the Forces. Now there was the chance that some lucky wives and mothers would have their sons and husbands returned because demobilisation was to begin on 16th June 1945.

It was on Sunday, 2nd September 1945 that Japan signed the document of final surrender. The school closed one day early for the mid-term break and the village held a Thanksgiving Week from 6th to 13th October.'

HIGHDAYS&HOLIDAYS

MAKING OUR OWN ENTERTAINMENT

There was little time for leisure, and few paid holidays, but most of us found entertainment in our own homes or villages in the past, when even the smallest place seemed to harbour local talent. Then there were evenings out at the cinema in town, or days out at the coast to look forward to, where the resorts had delights all their own.

▨ VILLAGE SOCIALS ▨

'I came to Dorset when my family were evacuated from London in 1940. The village we came to had socials, generally with local talent so after a few times of going you knew who was going to sing what! And where the flour bag was going to fall when "Sure a little bit of heaven fell from out the skies one day" rang out. Generally at the

Dorchester FC at the opening of their new pavilion in 1933.

interval the men retired to the local and weren't seen again that night at the village hall.'

THE GENTRY

'At village functions the front row was always kept for the "gentry" and everyone would rise as they came in, and not sit down until the front row was settled. This was in the 1920s.'

WE MADE OUR OWN ENTERTAINMENT

'Villagers made their own entertainment in the 1930s. We had no village hall in Stour Row until 1947, indoor events were held in the College Arms pub clubroom. This was mainly dancing, socials, concerts and whist drives. We had many locals with talent such as singers, a pianist, a mouth organ player, and a violin player. There was so much to do, we never got bored. Stour Row joined in local carnivals, always humorous. My parents were always in this and I always seem to be somewhere in the goings on. Outdoor events (before the war) included football, small fetes with children's games and tug-o-war and a few boxing bouts, but these did not last too long.

At home, we played cards, dice games and listened to the wireless. I spent a lot of time outdoors playing. Christmas was lovely; we had one, maybe two gifts and they were always hidden, with nuts, sweets and an orange by our bed. Father used to cook the chestnuts by the fire. My sister played piano, we would all sing and we played real party games. During the war we all used to walk to Shaftesbury picture house, and after we would buy some chips and walk home singing the three and a half miles. Mother always came. We only had two bikes.'

'At Corfe Castle between the wars our amusements were mostly self made, though there was a cinema in Swanage. We could hop on the train for eightpence return, and be there in ten minutes. There was a

Villagers gathered for a fete at Woodville Stour Provost.

cricket club, captained by the doctor, a small orchestra, and plays, whist drives and dances took place in the school hall as that was the only meeting place there was. At home we sat at the table round the oil lamp in the evenings, and played cards or dominoes, draughts or halma, or read, and in the summer time there was always plenty to occupy us out of doors.'

◈ An Evening's Entertainment ◈

'Mending on Saturday evenings, I remember sometimes Mother would unpack the old hand-operated, wooden-cased sewing machine (which had been her mother's) if there were quite a few patches needed for trousers (cotton drill) or milking overalls. Then there were piles of socks, "eaten" by wellington boots, cotton socks in summer, wool ones in winter. When teacher gave us a lesson in darning she took my "mend" to show her friend, as she could see

Bridport Ladies' Swimming Club camping at West Bay, 1945.

that I'd had plenty of practice! We also darned lisle or wool stockings and if there was a ladder we used a special hook and latch tool to pick it up.

While we worked our entertainment was *In Town Tonight*, a play, usually an hour and a half, and the news on the radio, run on a twelve volt dry battery, which lasted two to three months, and an accumulator glass-cased battery, needing recharging every week at the local garage, for 6d.'

◇ OUR BAND ◇

'Our band was formed in the early 1920s with the bandmaster the only member who could read music. He taught the others by playing the tune over and over until they could play "by ear". I remember them walking the main street of our village in the Blackmore Vale, dressed in their Sunday best – one wearing a smock – playing *Marching through Georgia*, the only tune they seemed to know. However, this small beginning was enough for gradually they progressed to win awards at the London contests. At the Jubilee in 1935 there were three generations playing together. They became the Silver Prize Band.

The church Youth Group was well supported each Monday evening. We played darts, dominoes, cards and once a month we had a dance or entertainment. Bill Waddington (Percy Sugden of *Coronation Street*) was one of our entertainers. He played his ukelele and sang George Formby songs. During the war our drama group entertained the searchlight batteries on the surrounding hills.'

▨ Our Annual Trip to Weymouth ▨

'In the 1950s and 1960s I can remember waiting with eager anticipation and great excitement for our annual summer trip to Weymouth on the paddle steamer. My brother and I would be up early and my mother would be busily preparing the picnic. We waited on the beach and watched the steamer coming into Lulworth cove. A long, narrow gangplank had to be wheeled on its huge cart wheels out into the water to meet the boat, which dared not come any nearer to the shore for fear of running aground. We clambered, single file, up the steep walkway and boarded the steamer at last. My mother, who was not a great lover of the sea, was always very anxious throughout the journey, and the children in her charge were all given strict instructions not to climb on the railings or go too near the edge. The steamer had to reverse out of the cove, and then we were on our way. My brother loved to go and look at the engine working. He seemed fascinated by the great pistons and other gleaming machinery.

At last we docked at Weymouth harbour and then proceeded to the beach. A sandy beach with shallow warm water was a treat for us and the thrill of a donkey ride over the golden sands followed by the Punch and Judy show was always a highlight. We

A busy day at Swanage Bay, from the Recreation Ground.

were not so impressed with the sandy sandwiches, but we didn't let that mar our day. There was still the journey home to look forward to!'

▓ ON THE BEACH AT BOURNEMOUTH ▓

'I was born in Bournemouth in 1907 in Charminster Road, which was the outer edge of Bournemouth then. My father was a baker and a confectioner. We had a shop in Charminster Road.

Bournemouth had a beautiful wide sandy beach then, starting from Hengistbury Head to Sandbanks in Poole. On the beach in my young days would be wonderful bathing huts on wheels, from which we kids used to jump off when not in use. They were pulled down to the water's edge by donkeys, so that no one could see the ladies go in and out of the water, and then the huts would be pulled back again for the night, near the promenade. No one was allowed to undress on the beach, even the little children in those days. An inspector would walk along the beach keeping his eyes open for the offenders. Rowing boat races and swimming races used to be held between Bournemouth and Boscombe Piers.

My grandfather (Henry Frodsham) had one of the very first shops in Bournemouth. He came from London in the year 1861. At what became Beale's Bookshop, my grandfather ran a restaurant and Beale's was just a newsagent's and sold buckets and spades. Grandfather also had a baker's and confectioner's shop near the Triangle where my father and his youngest brother were born. There were six sons.

The Frodsham brothers, when they grew up, ran the restaurants each side of Bournemouth Pier and the restaurant in the Golf Pavilion in Meyrick Park. My father as a baker and confectioner made all the food in the cafes.

My mother used to help in the cafes in August when they were very busy and I would be dumped on the beach to play by myself, although I was only about five years old. You can't imagine a mother doing that today. Then Bournemouth Corporation came along and ended my uncles' leases of the restaurants and deprived them of their living, so they went off to America to make their fortunes, just my father staying behind, all because my uncles, being very religious, wouldn't open on Sundays.

One of my earliest memories is of the bathchairs wheeling people about Bournemouth Gardens. Bournemouth was famous as a health resort. One part of the gardens behind the bandstand is still known today as the Invalid's Walk or the Pine Walk as there were so many pine trees which were supposed to be good for people suffering from chest complaints.

Another memory is a huge dead whale which was washed up onto the beach near the pier. Hordes of people came to see it and it stank to high heaven after a few days.

One of the memories I treasure is of the old pier, which was blown up in 1940 after Dunkirk to stop the Germans landing. I used to see as many as five pleasure steamers moored alongside the pier, two each side and one at the end. There was the *Balmoral*, the *Bournemouth*

Queen, the Lorna Doone, the Empress of India, the Lord Elgin, the Monarch and the Majestic. They used to be packed in the summer, particularly on bank holidays. We used to have lovely trips to Swanage, round the Isle of Wight, Weymouth, Lulworth Cove (only the Lorna Doone could get into Lulworth as the entrance to the cove was so narrow and she was the only small boat which could manage it), also to Torquay and Cherbourg, 2s 6d first class and 1s 6d second class to Swanage. These boats went to the assistance of the troops at Dunkirk.

There was a man called Bill Bailey, a photographer who used to stand on the pier and blow a whistle at the trippers on the boats to call their attention and then take their photographs and sell them the photos on their return. He must have made a lot of money.

On lovely summer evenings, my dad and I would go down on Bournemouth pier and listen to the band and watch the ladies and gentlemen all dressed up in their wonderful evening clothes and jewellery, coming out of their hotels and parading up and down the pier – just to show off their clothes I suspect.

There were pierrots down on the beach beside the pier on the east side playing to packed audiences and further along by the West Cliff Lift were the Gay Cadets. I used to sit on the railings as a kid every day when Mum was working in the cafe and listen to them. I never put a penny in the bag they brought round, but I learnt a lot of old songs.

Then there was an Italian selling the first ice creams we ever saw, ½d cornets and 1d wafers sold on the beach near the pier, Valeto ice creams I think they were called.

One summer night there was a terrible storm. All the deckchairs were blown out to sea, the bathing huts and beach bungalows were badly damaged and some washed out to sea. The Gay Cadets lost their piano which was washed up on Swanage beach. There used to be a third pier at Southbourne, but it was wrecked in a storm in 1900.

In the winter my father used to take me to the old Bournemouth Gardens (a glasshouse like the old Crystal Palace) long before the modern Winter Gardens or the BIC were built. Sir Dan Godfrey used to conduct the Bournemouth Municipal Orchestra, as it was called then, in the old Winter Gardens. I can't imagine teenagers going out with Daddy on Saturday nights nowadays, but it gave me a great love of classical music for which I am very grateful. Charles Groves was also a conductor. During the interval there was always a star turn: Harry Lauder, George Robey, Kathleen Ferrier, Gracie Fields, Nelly Wallace and others. People used to walk around the balconies while concerts were taking place. You can't imagine that going on during the Proms at the Albert Hall. I believe Edward Elgar conducted his own music there too.

In the summer the Municipal Brass Band used to play on the pier, Sir Dan Godfrey's son conducting. I can quite clearly remember a blind pianist being led on to the platform to play, there were no guide dogs then. There were concert parties performing on the pier then too.

There used to be rollerskating on the end of the pier and a lot of fishing was done from the landing stage. I don't think I should like to have eaten those fish, there where all the boats used to come in and out. I can well remember the horrible jellyfish that surrounded the pier, you could see their bright little eyes shining in the sun.

There used to be seats all around the pier where you could sit and enjoy the sun and sea air, today they have taken nearly all of them away and charge for a deckchair.

Coming down Richmond Hill the old trams often used to run off the lines at the bottom of the hill and run nearly across Bournemouth Square. We children used to watch fascinated as the men worked to get the trams back on the line up the hill. There was a terrible tram accident just below the Triangle opposite the back of what is now Marks and Spencer, in 1908. The brakes failed and the tram ran down the hill and plunged over the rails of the upper gardens, a very deep drop, which had been known as the fairy glen. Many lives were lost and many injured.'

Royal Days

Since the days of Queen Victoria, towns and villages across Dorset have celebrated Royal jubilees and coronations with great enthusiasm. Of the hundreds of local memories, these are just a few.

❖ Queen Victoria's Jubilee in 1887 ❖

'My father's most outstanding memory was Queen Victoria's Jubilee in 1887. "I was nine years old, and something seemed to be taking place all that summer. We were always lining up for one thing or another, and usually got a bun and an orange each. All the Sunday schools got together for a Sunday school treat, and it was held in a field at Bampton, on a slope facing Joby Legg's brewery. I won the race for boys under nine and was awarded a Jubilee sixpence, and as soon as I gave it to my mother, she was offered 2s 6d for it.

'If that's the worth of it. I'll keep it for Fred,' my mother said, and refused to part with it. They were all called in a few days later, because they were the same size and pattern as a half-sovereign, and some wise boy had started to gild them. My mother kept mine for years, and was always proud to show it; but when she grew old, she was cheated into parting with it."'

'All the women in the land contributed towards the Albert Memorial for the Queen's Jubilee. Shillingstone ladies all paid one penny each and had a hand-written letter from the Queen, dated 22nd June 1887, thanking them:

"I am anxious to express to all the women of Great Britain and Ireland how *deeply* touched and gratified I am by their very kind and generous present. I thank them most warmly for it, and shall value their gift of the statue of my beloved husband very highly – as a touching remembrance of this interesting and never to be forgotten day and of their great loyalty and affection."'

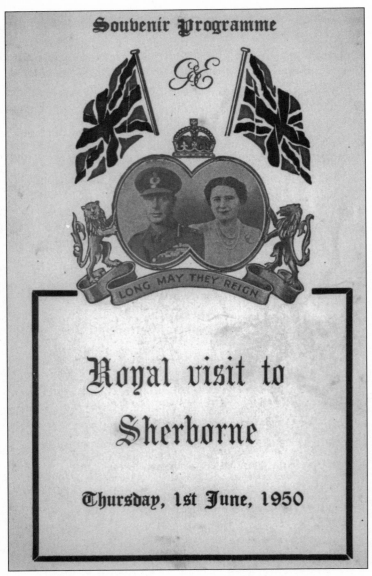

Souvenir Programme

Royal visit to Sherborne

Thursday, 1st June, 1950

A record of the Royal visit to Sherborne in 1950.

JUBILEE AND CORONATION

'For the 1935 celebrations for George V's Jubilee in Bournemouth, a villager from Alderholt attended with friends. She remembers buying a silver grey flannel suit from Swan and Edgar's for £2.

For the Queen's Coronation in 1953 there were great celebrations at the Old School at Alderholt.'

'The 1935 Jubilee was celebrated at Chedington with sports and tea and a bonfire in the evening. All the children under 14 years of age were given a mug by Sir Henry Peto who lived at the Court. The coronation in 1937 of George VI was much the same – sports, tea and bonfire, but we were given a spoon this time. The 1953 Coronation was celebrated with sports and a bonfire in the village.'

'At West Lulworth there were fetes with a fancy dress parade for special occasions such as the 1935 Jubilee. I can remember George V visiting Bovington and Lulworth camps and the schoolchildren walked up to see him. For the Jubilee, the pupils of the village school were dressed as children of the Commonwealth. A competition was held for the best decorated house or cottage and in the evening there was a bonfire on Hambury Tout. The same thing happened for the Queen's Coronation in 1953 but then the bonfire was held on Bindon Hill. All the village children were given mugs to celebrate these Royal events.'

THROUGH THE YEAR

Every year the time came around for the fetes and fairs, sports and regattas that were such high spots on everyone's calendar, as well as traditional celebrations such as Christmas festivities.

THE FETE AT SUTTON POYNTZ

'One of the highlights of village life was the annual fete of the Slate Club Sick Benefit. How the children loved the fair, the steam engines,

STUDLAND
JUBILEE CELEBRATIONS

Dear Sir or Madam,

At a General Meeting of Villagers held on March 18th, an Organising and Finance Committee of 12 members was elected to arrange how this village might suitably commemorate the Jubilee.

The Organising Committee met on March 25th and after considering the many suggestions made at the General Meeting decided on the following tentative action.

Studland May 6th.

The Village to be decorated with flags and bunting.

11.30 a.m. Public Relay of Broadcast Thanksgiving Service in St. Paul's Cathedral, London.

2.30 p.m. Special Combined Service in the Parish Church.

3.15—4.45 p.m. Sports of all kinds for all ages, with numerous prizes.

5.0 p.m. Gala Tea for all Schoolchildren. Also separate Gala High Tea for all Villagers, aged 65 and over.

8.30 p.m. Open Air Dance.

All children in the Village to be presented with special Jubilee Commemoration Mugs.

A permanent Memorial to be erected, the form of which is still under discussion, but which will probably consist of a stone, oak or teak seat, and/or the planting of trees at some useful spot in the village.

Lastly it is hoped to make a substantial subscription on behalf of the Village towards the Prince of Wales Youth of England Scheme, which H.M. the King has chosen as the most suitable personal gift to himself.

The Organising Committee consists at present of Mrs. Cowie, Mr. Harvell, Mr. A. Horlock, Canon Jaques, Mr. Jenkins, Mr. Eddie Loveless, Mr. A. G.

Studland celebrated the Royal Jubilee and Coronation in the 1930s.

Bridport Royal Charter Pageant

1253   1953

SOUVENIR 1/- PROGRAMME

June 24th—June 27th, 1953

The programme for Bridport's 700 year celebrations in June 1953,
Coronation year.

Cooks, waitresses and helpers at a Club Day dinner at Litton Cheney in the 1920s.

the roundabouts and "Peggy O'Neil" being played. One penny, or two at most, provided a lovely ride. Then there were sports of all kinds – simple pleasures were enjoyed in those days.'

▨ A Pig for a Song ▨

'In the 1930s we had many enjoyable evenings with Dad playing his accordion or squeezebox. We would sing away happily. Dad sang at a fair near our home at Acton, and won the pig. He hadn't anywhere to put it so it ended up in Granfer's quarry shed and after that Dad set up a sort of smallholding with pigs, geese, chickens and vegetables.'

▨ The Constabulary Sports ▨

'The great event of the year in Dorchester was the Dorset Constabulary Athletic Club Sports which was held every June at the recreation

At a local fair in the 1930s, an Acton man sang for a pig and won it!

Carnival time in Dorchester in the 1930s.

ground in Weymouth Avenue. There were club events for members of the Force, and open events which attracted competitors from all over the country.

One club event was a cycle race for policemen using their own upright type bike which had to weigh not less than 35 lbs. In the open cycle race one famous competitor was Bill Harvele who represented Great Britain at the Olympic Games.

As well as track events, running, walking and cycling, there was also the high jump and an obstacle race. Tug of war attracted police teams from many other forces who came regularly each year to compete.

This was a great day when friends came to lunch and we all hurried to the sports field by 1.30 pm to take our seats in the grandstand. There were stands of various types around half the circular arena. Trains travelling past on the eastern side slowed down, or stopped for passengers to view the activities. There was so much to watch as various entertainments were taking place, pillow fighting on a greasy pole, clowns and stilt walking, while a military band provided background music.

Behind the stands were many marquees, in the largest all the prizes were on display, mirrors, armchairs, clocks, canteens of cutlery and many other items. One wonders how much they cost then, and what would be the price today. There were tents for competitors, officials, and other services, and the well patronised refreshment tent.

The programme of events kept us riveted to our seats, a loudspeaker announced each event, and later the winner. There was great excitement as we watched special friends compete. In earlier years my father, who was a runner, won a clock; today in its ornate wooden case it hangs on the wall in the hall, a reminder of days long ago.'

⊠ THE YEAR AT WEST LULWORTH ⊠

'Throughout the seasons life, it seems, revolved around the fairs. Horses would be let out of their winter stables on 14th May – Wool Fair, and brought in on 21st September – Woodbury Hill Fair. This was an indicator of the short spell of warm nights.

Village treats were a once-a-year trip to the seaside with the Sunday school. The local inn was very much the "social club" for men only, where, no doubt, farming and gambling were the main topics of conversation. Each village had its resident policeman, mobile on his push bike.

Bonfire Night was when the common would be set alight, burning off the furze and leaving the black stalks for future firewood.

Harvest Service always saw a full church, with all the produce being sent to a local hospital.

West Lulworth used to have a Mummers play called *The Battle of Waterloo* which was performed every Christmas Eve at various houses in the village and also going "over the hill" to Tyneham House. The Mummers were a group of eight men, six of whom were dressed in white suits decorated with bright coloured tinsel, ribbons and glass etc. The other two men took the part of the Doctor/Horse and Father

Morris dancers at Redway Corner, Litton Cheney in the 1940s.

Christmas. The play was performed until the 1914–18 war. It was never written down but just passed on by word of mouth to each generation. With the outbreak of war someone must have had the foresight to write it down, because in the 1960s a copy was given to me. Our WI performed a small part of this play at one of our Christmas parties.

Memories of Christmas festivities at the turn of the century: "Two principal men led the procession right through the village, always dressed as old fashioned farmers. As they did so, they did an old fashioned broom dance and others joined in behind them so that soon nearly all the young, and not so young, joined in and it looked really good. As they passed the private houses, they sang carols and with everyone joining in you could hear them in Wool! In those days there were always a beer barrel outside a lot of the places and, by the time they had finished, they hardly knew what was going on. But the villagers really enjoyed it. In those days, we all mucked in with mouth organs, bugles or anything that would make a noise. They were out for enjoyment, and that they did. Some had hoes, spades and saucepans and it was really exciting. But you must get two men or women who can lead the percussion and let rip all the time, for no noise means no fun."

In the 1930s I can remember the Sunday school outings to Weymouth and the Christmas parties held in the school or village hall. Christmas was a special time of the year when I was very young. My father would wait until we were in bed on Christmas Eve and then would begin to decorate the living room. We were amazed when we came down on Christmas morning to find the room full of holly and ivy, with oranges and apples hanging from strings. In our stockings there was one toy and some fruit and nuts. The magic was spoilt when I went to school, when the identity of Father Christmas was revealed to me by an older child!'

INDEX

221

LIST OF CONTRIBUTING INSTITUTES

Contributions have been received from the following Dorset Women's Institutes:

Alderholt Afternoon • Alderholt Evening
Beaminster Evening • Blackdown
Bothenhampton • Bothenhampton Evening
Bradford Abbas • Bridport Centre • Burton
Burton Bradstock • Cattistock • Charmouth
Child Okeford • Crossways • Dorchester Centre
Durlston • Gillingham • Halstock • Hazelbury Bryan
Holwell • Kinson • Lanehouse • Langton Matravers
Leigh • Lilliput • Lydlinch • Marnhull
Melbury Abbas & Cann • Milborne St Andrew
Milton on Stour • Mosterton Afternoon • Owermoigne
Portesham • Portland • Preston cum Sutton Poyntz
Puncknowle & Swyre • Rodwell
Spetisbury & Charlton Marshall • Stoborough • Stours, The
Studland • Sutton Waldron & Iwerne Minster
Swanage Evening • Symondsbury • Throop
Toller & Hooke • Ulwell • Verwood Afternoon
Verwood Evening • West Bay • West Lulworth
West Moors Afternoon • Witchampton • Wool